The
ARTFUL
WOODEN
SPOON

The ARTFUL WOODEN SPOON

How to Make Exquisite Keepsakes for the Kitchen

JOSHUA VOGEL

Photographs by SETH *and* KENDRA SMOOT

CHRONICLE BOOKS

SAN FRANCISCO

*For my family, who have preceded and supported me in all things,
and who will eventually need to pick up where I have left off.*

Text copyright © 2015 by Joshua Vogel.

Photographs copyright © 2015 by Seth and Kendra Smoot.

Library of Congress Cataloging-in-Publication Data:

Vogel, Joshua.
  The artful wooden spoon : how to make exquisite keepsakes for the
kitchen / Joshua Vogel ; photographs by Seth and Kendra Smoot.
    pages cm
  Includes index.
  ISBN 978-1-4521-3772-8
1. Wooden spoons. 2. Wood-carving. I. Title.

  TT199.7.V64 2015
  736'.4—dc23

                        2015007841

Manufactured in China

Designed by Jennifer Tolo Pierce

10 9

Chronicle Books LLC
680 Second Street
San Francisco, California 94107
www.chroniclebooks.com

YOU CAN ALWAYS REMOVE MORE WOOD,

BUT YOU CAN'T PUT ANY BACK.

A SPOON *is a* SPOON *by* ANY OTHER NAME

English
SPOON

BASQUE
KOILARA

Latin
COCHLEARE

ARABIC
ملعقة

CANTONESE
匙

Dutch
LEPEL

FRENCH
CUILLÈRE

GERMAN
LÖFFEL

HAWAIIAN
PUNA

LUSIKKA
FINNISH

DANISH
SKE

Italian
CUCCHIAIO

Hebrew בכפית

HUNGARIAN KANÀL

Irish **SPÚNÓG**

NORWEGIAN SKJE

JAPANESE スプーン

Korean 숟가락

RUSSIAN Ложка

GREEK (MODERN) Κουτάλι

MANDARIN 勺子

SANSKRIT चमस

MONGOLIAN Халбага

Swedish SKED

Portuguese **COLHER**

HINDI चम्मच

Spanish **CUCHARA**

SCOTTISH/GAELIC SPÀIN

Turkish **KAŞIK**

URDU

CONTENTS

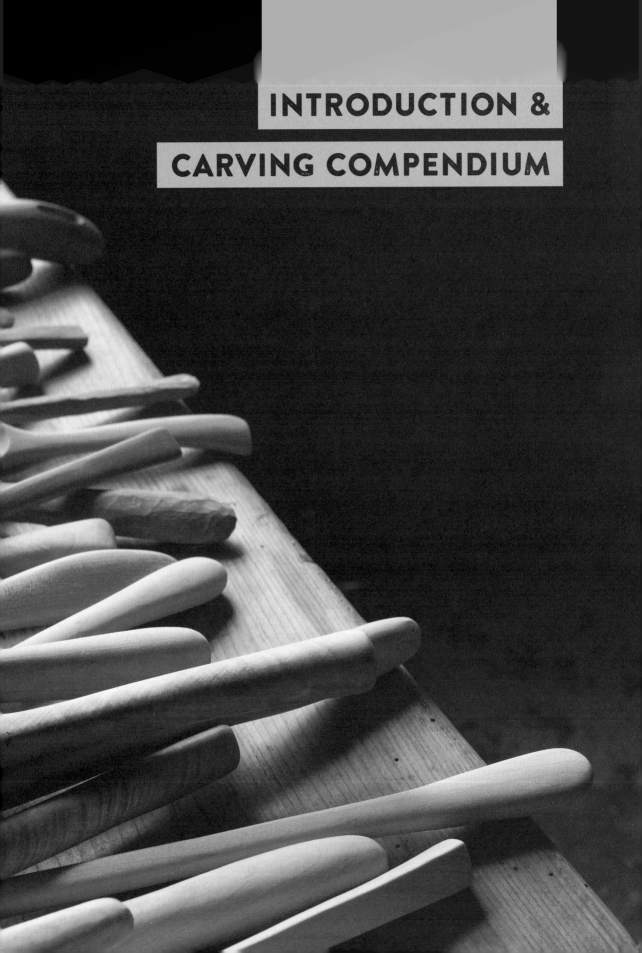

INTRODUCTION &
CARVING COMPENDIUM

The origin of carving predates written history. In fact, early peoples' carvings have provided the modern record with clues about our ancient beginnings. These artifacts speak for themselves across the millennia. How early people made things and what they made have become the subject of a great amount of modern thought about ourselves and our origins. Pinpointing the very beginning of carving and our relationship with it may well be fruitless (and is also beyond the scope of this book), but further investigating the pursuit of woodcarving and better understanding its origins and employment can only help in the search for answers to the questions that do much to define us today. This supposition is not only the basis of my work and my life's pursuit, but also suggests that making things by hand is a fundamental part of being human and not simply a contemporary craft movement.

Woodcarving is among the earliest of human vocations. And, as with most enduring human practices, woodcarving is multifaceted and deeply rooted across cultures. It is not only a creative expression, but also ultimately functional. Whether wood is carved to create something beautiful, such as for sculpture, or something primarily utilitarian, as in tool making, the craft, both past and present, reflects the warm glow of the creative spirit and carries with it the larger collective genius of the human species.

At a glance, an investigation of carving can help describe our relationship to the natural world and the wonderful variety of materials therein. When we use a material, we are bound to the laws of its characteristics. We develop tools and techniques to exploit its virtues and attempt to shape it to match our conceptions. The materials that we choose to use speak volumes about our particular environments at any point in time.

Our fundamental needs—food, clothing, and shelter—can describe categories of objects that are full of iconic forms that have come to us through our rich woodworking history. There is the spoon and bowl, the loom and spindle, the roof overhead, and even doors, which, simple though they may all be, embody our needs and the history of our humanity. While it may be easy to take some of these items for granted, it is our exploration and re-exploration of their forms and cultural significance that makes these objects catalysts for moving forward as well as for better understanding the past.

A BRIEF HISTORY OF THE SPOON

Common belief holds that spoons or spoonlike tools have been in active use since the Paleolithic era; that is, since the Stone Age. But what do we mean when we say "spoon"? The functionality of the bowl of a spoon suggests that it is to be used to collect or scoop what we might have trouble picking up or manipulating with our fingers alone. A handle, allowing maneuverability, leverage, control, and distance, is another requisite part. Together, the bowl and the handle create a unique form we know to be widely employed for all things culinary, from measuring, mixing, and preparing to serving and, of course, eating. But are these the only uses for a spoon or just the ones that we are familiar with?

A spoon-shaped implement was discovered in Avdeevo, a site located near Kursk in the central Russian plain that was found below a layer of sediment known to have been deposited more than twenty thousand years ago. The tool seems to be a partially modified piece of mammoth ivory, the bowl being accentuated by an abrasive or scratching action. What this object was actually used for is purely a matter of speculation. That it is a specialized combination of concave and convex surfaces with a handle, and that it was a tool that was well used by early humans at least fifteen thousand years before the advent of written history, is a matter of evidence. What might our Stone Age, hunter-gatherer ancestors have needed such a tool for? Excising bone marrow, cleaning game, or perhaps preparing skins? Whatever the use or uses, the spoon's shape is still recognizable and purposeful and helps to explain why spoons are among our earliest tools.

Further investigation of the archaeological record tracks the form through the millennia. By the early to middle Neolithic period, sites such as Starčevo in the central Balkans, which has been dated back to around 6000 BCE, have turned up spoonlike tools along with other bone and stone implements such as awls, needles, burnishers, scrapers, chisels, wedges, and axes. The wear patterns on spoons from these Neolithic sites suggest that they may have been used on soft organic material such as animal hides and plant fibers, perhaps to mix and apply pigments or prepare leather. We can only speculate on the exact use of these surviving implements, but the Starčevo archaeological finds suggest a degree of material specialization, industry,

and ornamentation that counts spoons as both a unique and a well-used tool shape in an epoch that is widely considered to be the dawn of civilization.

The earliest surviving wooden spoon may well be Egyptian, which is not to say that earlier people did not make these shapes in wood, but simply that surviving evidence of wood examples seems to enter the archaeological record during the early Bronze Age between three thousand and four thousand years ago. Dry, sealed tombs have preserved wooden implements and furniture that would have ordinarily disintegrated over time, providing us a rare glimpse into the distant past. Examples of early Egyptian wooden spoons have been painstakingly carved in the most delicate manner, with the handle often made to represent a person or an animal. Complex wooden sculptures known as "swimming spoons" start to be found in funereal inventories of the time. These sculptural spoons usually depict a highly stylized, anthropomorphic figure, prone (as if swimming) and holding a bowl or basket shape with outstretched arms. Trace amounts of materials found on the spoons indicate that these implements were used not for food but rather for holding cosmetics.

Many of these Egyptian examples have exquisite lids that were designed to pivot open or closed. Other theories suggest the spoons were used as ritual offering utensils, such as to measure and scoop incense. Here again, the exact use of the spoon is only speculative; that the tools have the requisite bowl and handle, and have been fashioned with great artistry and care, indicates the continued importance and evolution of the form.

Iron Age wooden spoons have been found preserved in peat bogs, dating to between two thousand and three thousand years ago at the Rathcroghan site in what is now modern-day Ireland. Some of these well-preserved wooden implements were found with traces of butter still on them, which makes the way that these tools were used much easier to know!

It is well documented that by Roman times distinct spoon shapes were being used to suit different types of food. *Ligula*, or tongue-type, spoons were developed for serving and eating soft foods and soups, and *cochlearium*, or shell-type, spoons were used specifically for eating shellfish or eggs.

During the Middle Ages wooden spoons are found to be ubiquitous in most if not all woodworking cultures of the time. One of the most enduring wooden spoon–making traditions that is still practiced in much the same way today as it was many centuries ago comes to us from Scandinavia. A one-thousand-year-old tool chest found by a farmer tilling soil in Mästermyr, Sweden, revealed a tool kit that bears a striking resemblance to the tool collection depicted in this book. This at least points to the idea that much of what we are capable of carving today was not only possible but also probable one thousand years ago.

Most major civilizations, in both the East and West, have their own words and traditions for making and using spoons. The humble spoon is pedestrian, perhaps, but only in the noblest sense of the word, and can be regarded as both a sculptural and sophisticated tool developed over thousands, if not tens of thousands, of years. And while the spoon's basic purpose may be self-evident, it still takes great skill and patience to conceive and requires a sufficient mastery of craft to execute.

The spoon stands out as a unique turning point in tool specialization and is a distinct hallmark of civilization. It can be base and elegant at the same time, both immediately recognizable and useful. The form is so pervasive and strong that it has allowed for an almost endless degree of design application, both utilitarian and artistic alike. Indeed, the spoon must be recognized as one of the oldest, most universally understood possessions.

I regard the making of wooden spoons as a kind of functional sculpture. The challenges in making them are the same today as they were for our ancestors. In a classic sculptural sense, the process is wholly reductive, meaning that rather than adding bits or compiling parts, the wooden spoon's form is arrived at by only removing material. It comes to life or is revealed by taking away all the material that is *not* the spoon (referred to as "stock removal"). A carved spoon is a single piece of wood that is made dynamic through this intensive process. Taken alone, this would make wooden spoons sculpturally unique, but that they also serve a purpose beyond their form is, I believe, what can make them exceptional.

THE COMPENDIUM

This compendium is a visual invitation to explore spoon making, the process of wood sculpture, and the idea that the work itself can become a

creative meditation. It is a collection of thoughts, actions, and ideas as well as objects. It is as much about the intention and the tools behind the work as it is about the spoons themselves. I offer these thoughts as an open-ended exploration of the language of shapes and function, of the contemporary design process, of problem solving, and of diversion as well as occupation.

As I began work on the pieces for this compendium, I had a sense that the form was intriguing, but I wasn't expecting to discover such a far-reaching and fundamental connection with the work. A twenty-thousand-plus-year history is a challenging amount of time and history to try to absorb.

We may take for granted that the utensils that we use have always existed, but not all of them are really that old. The fork, it turns out, is a relatively new addition to our table, having come into use during the Roman Empire. The spoon is in another category altogether. People have been making spoons for a long, long time. Understanding their shape and purpose must certainly be in our blood. The reoccurrence of the tool itself throughout history says a lot about our collective lifestyle and our natural instincts.

As far as tool making goes, carved spoons are proletarian in nature, never really considered high art, but certainly revered and necessary all the same. Spoons are in effect enduring sculpture by the people for the people. The shape itself is understandable to even the smallest child. We all have some intrinsic feeling of what is and is not a spoon, what a spoon should be, and how it will work. So the shape, its history, and how it is made are all accessible on many different levels. Spoon carving is the kind of work and craft that is ecumenical; everyone is capable of understanding and appreciating it.

Creating the spoons for the compendium generated over one hundred examples made from six basic types of wood (ebony, holly, cherry, white oak, maple, and apple), all unique in form and their use of the material. I tried to vary the shapes and techniques according to the properties of the wood. And I tried to use this variety as a way to explore the history of spoon forms, spoon making, and some tools that can be used to make spoons.

I have been carving spoons for some time now, and prior to writing this book, I lamented one aspect of my happy success: because all the spoons I made were finding their way out into the world, I had no way to regard them as a group, en masse. It isn't that I haven't enjoyed each spoon on an individual basis, or that I had stopped learning about making them as I made each one, but simply that I wanted to see them all together, to see how they related to one another. I wanted to be able to reflect. I wanted to find the shapes that I was forgetting about and to trace the narrative threads throughout the work to better learn the language that was developing with each additional spoon I made. Something captivated me about the idea of creating such an abundance.

When the opportunity arose to consider the spoons work as a larger, more cohesive investigation into the form of this iconic wooden utensil, I embarked on the idea of producing this carving compendium with great excitement and curiosity. How many more spoons would I need to make to feel comfortable writing about them? Ten? Twenty? Thirty? One hundred? What makes spoons special and worth the focus? What is the difference between a spoon and a spatula? When does a spoon become a ladle? Does a spoon even need to be useful to be a spoon? What does "handmade" mean? And "craft"? All these questions and more came along with the idea of creating the work for this compendium.

How do we begin to consider such a disparate collection? Let's begin with the idea that there is no one right way to do this work. Suspend the notion that there must be absolutes or that our labors will be wasted if they don't necessarily match our preconceptions. And most important, let's remind ourselves that there is an inherent joy in making things. Suppose that we might actually be able to surprise ourselves creatively, if we are able to give in to a process wholly. And that it is okay to follow our hearts to make decisions even if we don't know what the outcome will be in the end. We should be able to allow ourselves to be guided by our feelings and recognize them as some of our most important tools. Embrace the notion that the journey is indeed as important as reaching the destination and that learning is a unique pursuit in and of itself. Let's not be satisfied by engaging our minds only, but seek to include our bodies and spirits as well. Let's enjoy ourselves.

Think about balance as an active idea, not a passive one. If nurtured within, this potential awakening and interchange, all these concessions, could spark a fire that might just last a lifetime. Let's be open to all this and begin in this way.

CRAFT

Consider the notion of craft as an intermediary or a vehicle. It is important to think about it as expression and as a living part of culture, not an unnecessary tradition and certainly not merely a distraction. Craft can carry a high degree of refinement and promote a sophisticated understanding of our natural world. Pursuit of such understanding can make this work a cultural bridge with the ability to describe and shape disparate parts of our greater self-understanding. It can become a way to both mark and experience time, as in the Bronze Age or the Iron Age. It creates context that helps us reconcile both our natural and social surroundings and can be seen as a lens through which to consider the nature of progress.

Think about craft as a way to communicate and connect—not just with ourselves in the workshop but also on social and generational levels. How do we understand and express ourselves better simply by making

something? The real motivation behind my compendium lies in this search for the heart of craft.

WHY HANDMADE

Making things by hand is one of the best ways to directly access the heart of craft, although the definition of "handmade" is not as clear as it might seem. All craft requires tools, even the most rudimentary, so imagining "handmade" to mean "made particularly and exclusively by hand" is an unrealistic definition. Carving a spoon with a knife and a gouge is decidedly a handmade process, but what about using a bandsaw?

There is the sentiment that handmade items are distinguished by their process. Handmade objects require a personal and active transformation of basic materials and a soulful connection of the craftsperson with the world at large through the meditative aspect of the work. This act of discovery helps shape the object, so that the unique connection that the artisan had with the original material is passed along in the characteristics of the finished object.

The purposeful application of head, heart, and hands is what "handmade" is all about. Put differently, it is about the projection of the human spirit. The meditation of doing is a way of thinking about applying yourself to a handmade process. So we do things, we meditate, we make objects and artworks, we build stuff over and over, and we reflect on the work, only to make it anew and hopefully fresh. Why? I believe in the importance of objects that support and enhance our lives, but I also believe that this very act of creation itself can be supportive. I have a need to make things that goes well beyond my understanding of why I do it, but I also know that the closer I can get to my work, the more rewarding the work can be. I like to believe that there is some part of me that remains in everything that I have ever made.

So, what is not handmade? Where do we draw the line? Handmade items cannot easily be mass-produced. They are special and unique by nature. The distinction to me lies, partially, in the manner of tooling. Some people draw the line with tools that need power to operate. I subscribe to the idea that the tools that are employed to hand-make things have no logic of their own. The limits that are set are arrived at solely by the craftsperson's judgment, not a program or preconceived pattern or pathway. The processes are not general, and the point is not to *produce* but to *create*. Answer these questions when you assess whether an item qualifies as handmade: Does it have heart? Does it reflect a human quality and uniqueness beyond the material itself? If not, then it probably is not handmade.

There is a strong need for creative self-expression in today's world that can be exercised through this idea, perhaps more now than ever. Creativity is a lot more than just connecting things. Connection is the first step, but beyond that, creativity requires synthesis. It is what we do with the connections that really matters. We are beginning to reconnect with the importance of thoughtful food choices to nourish our bodies and in turn the importance of nourishment for our souls as a matter of well-being. Hand-making something can be another way to nourish ourselves; it inherently requires synthesis and includes creating a connection with both material and process. Through the effort we can exercise our ability to share on a number of levels, and revel in the challenge and the joy we get from doing so. At the core of all these connections is a message that says, "You are not alone."

HEIRLOOM?

Even if we endeavor to make beautiful, well-conceived work that we pour our hearts into, there is no guarantee that the object of our labors will stand the test of time. What if the work becomes antiquated, passé, broken, or lost? We don't have a crystal ball to look into the future to see what will be considered valuable, and for a number of other reasons, we really shouldn't suppose that what we make will become heirlooms. We should however strive to fight planned obsolescence, endeavor to build things to last, work with good intentions, and labor to instill the things that we make with those intentions. With luck, they *will* stand the test of time. In the end, the objects themselves are ephemeral. The real heirloom is the sentiment that an object carries with it.

WHY WOODEN SPOONS

As objects, wooden spoons are a beautiful use of a natural material employed for a specific function. I love that they have been used in cooking and to serve food for centuries, and longer, and are as useful in today's kitchens as they were in those of the past. I particularly love the idea that they can support the reality of daily chores in a soulful way and can help elevate the mundane to something special and even more enjoyable. I would venture to guess that the spoon is among the top ten most used tools in the world. It is ubiquitous, inherently understandable, and useful.

Some things get better with age, some things are best enjoyed in their prime, and there are definitely some things that are supposed to be handmade. I, for one, believe that there should be more handmade wooden spoons in the world that help connect people to their larger reality and, even more than this, that there could be more room for people who care to take the time to make them.

So the compendium is a compilation of all these things. It is a tribute to wooden spoons and a champion of the handmade; it is an investigation, an invitation, and an exploration. Mostly I offer it as a sincere and heartfelt thanks, and a handshake in thought to all the artists and craftspeople, now and generations before, who dedicate themselves to their work.

What follows is an in-depth look into the relationship between craftsperson, tool, and material, and an explanation of how these tools create the different types of curves that distinguish each spoon. There is a wide variety of tools and techniques available to the curious carver as well as a host of material choices, both found and commercially available. Any number of combinations are possible. And none is more correct than the other for making wooden spoons. Rather than dictating rules and narrowing the scope, let's explore.

The essence of spoon making is the orchestration of curves, transitions, and edges. Understanding the nature of making these shapes will help explain how to make the spoons themselves. Begin by dissecting the shape of a spoon in your mind, sectioning it into these categories: outside curves, inside curves, edges, and transitions. Each aspect relates to the other. The inside of the bowl is cradled neatly by the outside. The amount that the bowl will hold is, as it suggests, a balance in this relationship. The handle flows out of the bowl, and likewise, the bowl becomes an extension of the handle, which affects the overall shape and ultimately the way that a spoon can be used. The edges define the union between the curves.

The edge of the inside curve delineates the extent of the bowl shape; the edges of the outside curves flow outward to become the shape of transition.

A wooden spoon is a subtle balance between *convex* and *concave* surfaces. The spoon embodies and relies on both functioning at the same time to be successful. Try drawing the shape and you will discover how unique the form actually is. Where one curve stops, the other begins. Carving is no less exacting, perhaps even more so. The nature of each type of curve dictates the necessity of a particular tool. This is a very important point. It is this distinction that makes spoon work much more specific and specialized than simply whittling.

The first thing to understand about spoon carving is that you will need more than one type of tool to completely carve a wooden spoon. I divide the work into different parts to more easily explain this need. Convex, or outside, curves require a flat blade; concave, or inside, curves require a curved blade.

OUTSIDE CURVES

The spoke shave, straight knives, rotary tool, draw knife, ax, and flat and round files make up the bulk of the hand tools in the outside curves kit. Saws are also invaluable sculptural tools. Bandsaws and frame saws help in removing large portions and are both uniquely helpful for cutting curves.

Rounded, gibbous, outwardly curving, lenticular, umbellate, hogged, or convex surfaces are what we work on first. They are surfaces that can be

HAND TOOL KIT

flat and round files

spoke shave

frame saw

rotary too

ax

straight knives

draw knife

worked with a flat edge, an ax, a saw, or even a knife, for example. A single cut with a flat-edged tool will produce a flat planar surface, or facet. A number of facets, taken together, around a focal point will start to form a curve. Imagine a cube. In your mind's eye, begin to cut off each corner. Keep cutting. Quickly you will notice how many more corners you have created just by removing the first eight. You will also begin to see the cube become a polygon, and then more and more the cuts reveal a shape that approaches a sphere—the epitome of outside curves.

Outside curves are worked with flat-edge tools. Tangential, glancing cuts remove the high points and facets of wood from the rough material. Carving strokes can be long, sweeping movements that start well beyond the curve. Repetitive straight cuts reveal the final shape underneath. With outside curves, we want to find the direction of the wood grain and cut "downhill"; that is, downward on a slope, generally from an area of larger-diameter wood grain to an area of a smaller one.

 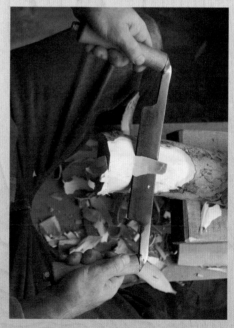

HAND TOOLS UP CLOSE (left to right): *Spoke shave and draw knife.*

INSIDE CURVES

Cupped, scooped, excavated, dipped, incurvate, crescentic, or concave surfaces are the yin to the yang of the outside curves. They form the part that will hold matter, the part that wants to accept, the scoop. As the name implies, inside curves mark the difference between what is inside a shape and what is outside. They are the types of curves that are themselves created with curved or domed implements, such as a gouge or a hook knife. Each cut of an inside curve tool makes a small "bite," or gouge, which creates new edges that allow consecutive cuts to be cumulatively productive. From an initial central cut or gouge, successive cuts radiate both outward from the center and inward ever deeper and wider. The cutting motion that produces inside curves is directed inward toward a fulcrum as opposed to a tangent. Again, one small curve made many times adds up to a bigger concave shape.

Inside curves are time-consuming to make, partially because the range of motion used to create them is more limited and focused than for outside curves. The size of the concave shape is also dictated by the size of the carving tool. Hollowing tools will generally

INSIDE CURVE TOOLS AT WORK (previous page): Hook knife. *(Left to right):* Spoon gouge and adz.

INSIDE CURVE TOOLS

hot iron

gouges

adz

rotary rasp

hook knife

spoon gouge

have a bent curve to better cut along inwardly sloping surfaces.

The phenomenon of the inside curve is that access becomes more restricted the deeper you get. The depth of a bowl shape can be no steeper than the steepest aspect of your gouge, and a large, wide, sweeping blade can't cut a small tight curve.

An abrasive approach may be among the first methods employed to create concave surfaces. A stone of the proper shape and coarseness, twisted repeatedly into a piece of wood, will create an inside curve. Rotary equipment can also be employed, as with most stages of carving, but the bit or head selection for concave work should be spherical or ovoid. What other methods might be used to create these shapes besides the conventional ones?

Aboriginal people of Australia have been known to use ants to help them hollow out objects by applying liberal amounts of honey to the areas they want to remove, which might be one of the more creative and interesting methods of stock removal. Burning may be one of the most basic and primal ways to create a concave shape in wood. Carving by burning is difficult to control (crude at best), time-consuming, and plausible only

CARVING BY BURNING (left to right): *Beginning to burn. Burning the bowl area and concaves.*

TOOLS *for* EDGES & TRANSITIONS

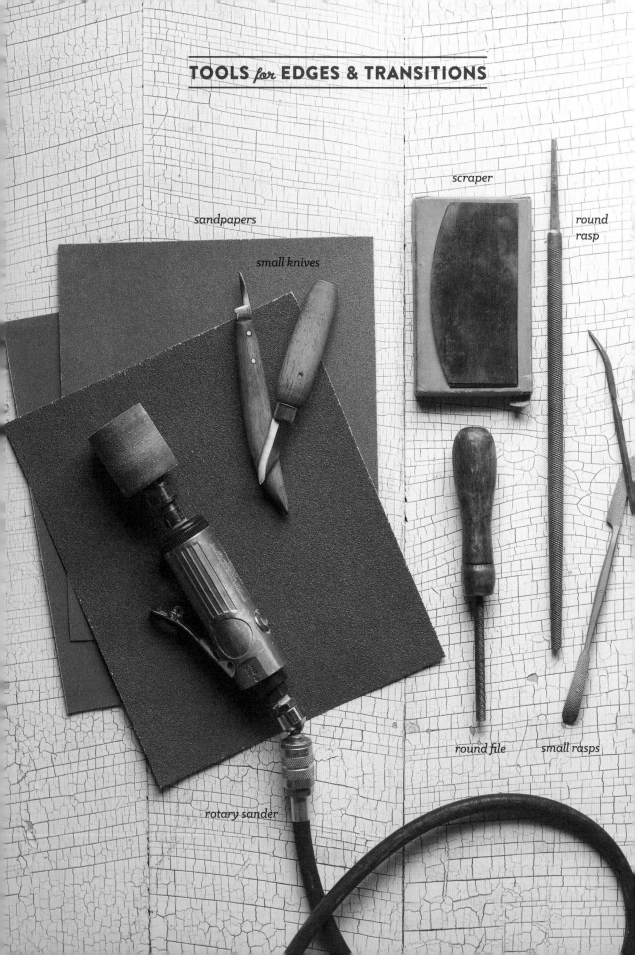

scraper

round rasp

sandpapers

small knives

round file

small rasps

rotary sander

if you have an extremely hot heat source. Carving with this method would be a very interesting challenge, but it is more just a romantic notion than an efficient technique.

EDGES AND TRANSITIONS

Some of the most overlooked aspects in carving—but also the most crucial, and the most telling—are edges where one surface starts and another stops, the valleys or ridges, corners, and seams. Edges can betray an imbalance between surfaces and highlight disparate shapes. Visually, they define the extent of surfaces, but they also help the mind envision the volume

that the finished spoon will be able to scoop and hold.

To the eye, edges are what divide light. They create shadows. How thin an object appears to be has everything to do with the edge that is presented. And the nature of the edge has everything to do with the presentation of the piece.

Defining edges and transitions as their own elements also helps direct attention and extra focus to these areas. Mostly, these elements are the product of other work. When you give these developing unions some special attention, you'll exult in the results.

EDGES AND TRANSITIONS (left to right): Bowl transitions to handle. Edge defines the shape of the bowl.

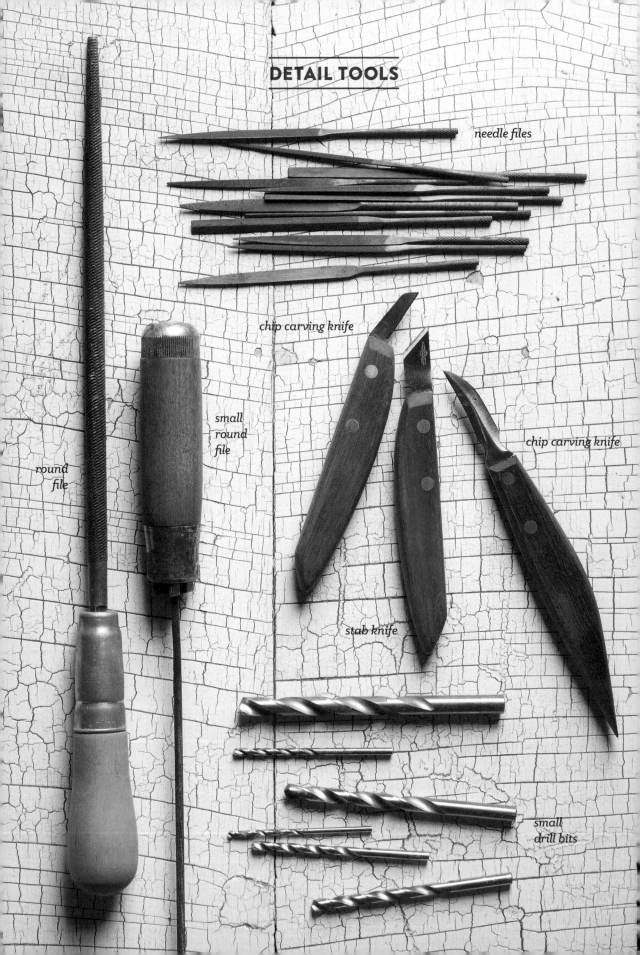

DETAIL TOOLS

needle files

chip carving knife

chip carving knife

round file

small round file

stab knife

small drill bits

Sweeten up the curve, ease the transition, and sharpen the line. Much of the time, edge work points out the need to resolve surface work.

DETAILS AND ORNAMENTATION

Ornamentation is described loosely as the act of decorating to make more attractive. But why can't detail become a textural change in surface, or the way an object hangs be thought of as ornament?

I have never liked gratuitous ornamentation. To me, ornamentation for the sake of decoration is a thin attempt to add interest to something that may not have needed it in the first place. I don't believe that any amount of embellishment can cover up a bad form. As well, a good shape can easily become obscured by embellishment. What is the whole point of ornamentation anyway?

Certainly the idea of ornamentation is to make an object more beautiful, but I think that beauty should find its way from the inside out, not be constructed from the outside in. And like any other design consideration, how ornament is added should have some inner logic or motivation. In this sense, ornamentation, to me, always

makes more impact when it can be a part of something useful, born out of need. The way a handle terminates or how an object hangs or is connected to another one are great examples of moments to be celebrated. That these moments can be considered ornamentation defies the idea of ornament as superficial and poses it as integral or, inversely, suggests that the object itself can become the ornament.

So beyond the idea of embellishment and making a beautiful object more beautiful, ornamentation, as surface treatment, can also be thought of as a way to further differentiate or personalize similar objects. *Chip carving* and *kohlrosing* are ancient techniques for carving ornamentation in wood, especially on spoons and similar utensils. Chip carving uses simple knife cuts to remove small predictable wedges of wood. Many such cuts work together in a pattern or rhythm to form an overall design or effect. Kohlrosing uses stab cuts that displace rather than remove wood fibers. Incised designs are made up predominantly of geometric repetitions such as cross-hatching or weave patterns, which are filled with pigment to accentuate the design.

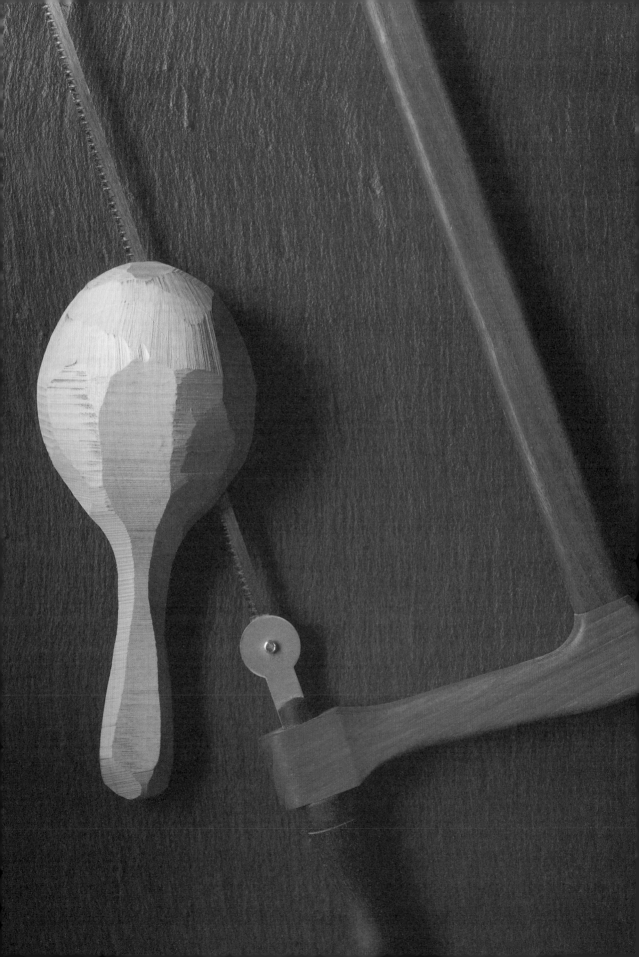

PRACTICAL SPOON-MAKING

OVERVIEW

There are several main distinctions and practical considerations for spoon-making work. It's helpful to establish a few categories and some basic vocabulary prior to jumping in with both feet. These are all recurring concepts, which weave throughout this and subsequent chapters and and will come into play in your own investigations. Let's lay some groundwork to help better understand and direct the discussion and the future choices we can make.

CHOOSING THE MATERIAL

What type of material should you choose to use in spoon making? Not all wood is created equal. In fact, there is great variation in species of trees and the quality of material to be found within them. Some wood is extremely dense and hard. In fact, there are several types of wood, such as ironwood and ebony, that are so dense that they sink in water. In contrast, some wood is very soft, fibrous, and buoyant, like balsa or linden. Despite its lightness, pound for pound, balsa ranks among the strongest woods in the world. With so much variation in material, not only are there many types of wood to choose from, but also we can afford to be choosy in making our selection. So when I describe wood as a "dense, closed-grain hardwood," what do I mean? It may be a bit misleading, but the standard vocabulary used to refer to the lumber from any deciduous tree is "hardwood," while all coniferous

trees are said to be "soft." Deciduous trees lose their leaves seasonally; conifers are evergreens, usually with needles rather than leaves. This is misleading because not all hardwood is hard (for example, balsa), nor is all softwood soft.

What about grain? What do we mean when we talk about wood grain? Visually, grain looks like the lines of a topographical map that describes the inner contours and growth patterns of the tree that the wood has come from. Practically, we use the term to be able to discuss both the character and quality of wood and also the direction in which we work with the wood. More than a mere visual characteristic, the grain describes the anatomy of a specific tree and delineates the seasonal growth of a tree. During the spring and summer months, a tree flush in all its foliage acts like a giant water pump, drawing moisture and nutrients out of the soil and up into the leaves, where it is converted into food for growth powered by the sun. Growth in trees takes the form of an added layer of wood, which is ever expanding, shifting, and splitting just beneath the bark, and the bark becomes a protective covering for this volatile soft addition. With a change in the seasons and the arrival of colder weather, the pump slows down, growth stops, the bark that once was in motion now fuses to the new wood, known as the *cambium*, and the tree solidifies. Year after year, this rhythm of growth and solidification creates what we regard to be growth rings, which are in essence the grain of the tree.

The forensics of the grain can indicate whether there was a lot of rain in a season or if it was a dry year. Perhaps it may reveal that a tree survived a fire or even grew steadily into the wind. The grain traces the natural movement of the tree and how it has grown. It is much easier to understand this and work with this natural phenomenon than it is to try to impose a different shape on the inherent nature of the wood. Boards that have severe twists or bows to them likely came from parts of a tree that were growing in that way already, rather than from having been dried improperly. Once a tree is growing in

a certain fashion, it is very difficult if not impossible to convince it to do otherwise. With this in mind, you begin to understand the meaning of the popular adage "go with the grain" or inversely "go against the grain," both immensely important concepts in life but even more so in working with wood. As a woodworker, I look to the trees first for inspiration. I think that it is important to notice the way the trees grow and their shape, structure, and biology, and to consider their stories. Some trees have been around for quite some time. Imagine all that they have witnessed, all they have adapted to, and all the things they would have to say if only they could.

I enjoy using dense, closed-grain hardwoods for carving projects. Although almost any wood can be carved, scraped, and sanded, I think that dense, closed-grain wood is the material of choice for kitchen implements. Dense hardwoods generally hold edges and details during carving much better than softwoods. They better resist general wear, and their smooth, contiguous surfaces are easier to keep clean. Closed-grain woods exhibit less grain variation from season to season and are less resinous and less porous. Wood of

ANATOMY *of a* SPOON

handle

transition

edge

bowl

this type is generally less fibrous and easier to carve into smooth shapes than open-grained woods.

So in particular, what are some dense, closed-grain hardwoods that are suitable for carving spoons? Maple and birch are wonderful choices, and fruitwoods, such as olive, apple, and cherry, are all hardwoods that are a pleasure to carve and to use as a finished product. Yes, there are standards and traditional material choices, but more than being a rule, think of these examples as guidelines. I like to be more adventurous, and of course some trees, such as birch, may not grow in your area. Be motivated more by the sweet syrup that flows through maple, or the essence of the apple fruit, rather than by convention. Follow your nose, especially when making spoons. Spending an afternoon carving fresh-cut fruitwood is a gently perfumed task. And accidentally burning a cherry wood spoon while cooking on the stovetop is quite different and much less terrible than burning one made from ash (or, worse, plastic, with the acrid smoke that results).

Be open to other attributes that may be even more important than whether a wood has a closed grain or is deciduous or is generally suitable for carving. Spoons don't take a lot of time or wood to make, so experimenting with trimmings and scraps is encouraged. Perhaps you have a tree in your own backyard or someone special to you planted a tree many years ago. Regardless of the type of wood that is in these trees, your connection to them may trump other more suitable choices. You may find yourself attempting to make measuring spoons from trimmings from your grandmother's lilac bush, and although lilac is not that common in the woodshop, there are certainly no rules against using it. The work becomes much more meaningful when we develop these types of motivations and connections within it.

WET VERSUS DRY WOOD

Whether to use wet or dry wood is another major consideration in material selection. Wet (green) wood refers to wood that has been freshly cut from a tree or that has a very high

WET AND DRY WOOD: Wet (left) and dry (right).

moisture content. In understanding the difference it may be helpful to consider that the purpose of most wood inside a tree is to help move water up from the ground into the leaves. On a cellular level, wood is a lot like a sponge. In this process, saturation is the normal, living state of wood.

Green wood is dimensionally unstable because its volume reflects the amount of water trapped inside as well as the wood fibers themselves. Green wood is full and can be quite heavy; some pieces may be able to hold many gallons of water. As soon as a tree is cut, the cut-off portion begins to lose moisture and thus shrinks and changes shape as the inevitable drying process begins. Wood will continue to lose moisture until the internal content reaches equilibrium with its environment, at which point it is considered to have been air-dried. Sometimes the drying process is expedited, such as in a kiln, to reduce moisture content even further. Most commercially available lumber has been dried in this manner. Dry wood has already done most of its shrinking and settling.

What is the ideal moisture content for the would-be carver? Green wood is much, much easier to work

with using basic tools, such as a knife and gouge, than is dry wood. Try using a hook knife on a freshly split piece of green sugar maple and then on one that has been drying for a few years. The difference will be immediately evident. Entire traditions of woodcarving and implement making rely on green material to start. The retained water lubricates tools as they cut, reducing friction. Wet wood is still supple and easy to slice, split, or bend. Many blade-type tools were made for this type of wet work. In fact, some carving techniques and tools are downright impossible and totally frustrating to use with dry material. Green wood is much easier to work with using bladed tools, but (and this is the distinction) it must still go through dimensional changes and its curing or drying process after it has been shaped, which takes time.

Dry wood is much harder than green wood. With the heavy moisture gone, the wood fibers and connective lignin solidify. Although the result is a lighter material, dry wood is much harder than its saturated equivalent. Blades will still cut dry material—it just takes much more effort—whereas wet wood will yield large slicing curls right off the knife. Dry wood gives up only smaller chips. Most conventional woodworking uses dry wood because it is more stable, predictable, and suited to working with abrasives, such as rasps and sandpapers. Dry particles tend to stick or gum up much less than wet particles, making the use of these techniques possible. With the whole curing process accomplished, dry wood projects can also be finished and used immediately as soon as they are done.

So more than just relative moisture content, the discussion of wet versus dry material leads to differences in carving process and tool selection. A wet wood project may take the form of a tree branch that is worked with an ax and knives, while a dry wood spoon may be made from a piece of ebony that you have been saving for years, which will be sanded to a high polish. Wet wood can be worked prior to curing; dry wood is worked after curing.

BLADES VERSUS ABRASIVES

When beginning to discuss process, it's good to start by looking at two different approaches to working with wood. Both types of tools were found in ancient tool inventories, and there is evidence of both methods—cutting and abrading—in even the earliest archaeological records. One can only suppose that chronologically, it must have all begun with Stone Age abrasives in service of either great need or obsessive curiosity.

There are perhaps as many opinions about each approach as there are woodworkers. The blade approach advocates splitting and slicing wood fibers, as opposed to using abrasives, which tear or compress fibers. Edged tools like axes, knives, and gouges are used for the blade approach, and rasps, files, and sandpapers for the abrasive technique. Abrasives are much better suited to work dry wood. Blades are much better suited to work wet wood. Either process takes a graduated approach, meaning the first step is the gross removal of stock with larger or heavier equivalent tools, and gradually we refine our movement (and tool choice), taking less and less off as the shape begins to reveal itself, with ever more refinement via smaller and lighter tools, until finally there is no more material to remove.

Blades are elegant and precise. The slicing action of the blade approach leaves wood fibers cut and smooth. An "off the knife" finish is said to not need additional oil or other protective coating because the surface is so smooth and stain-resistant. Work done against or through the grain,

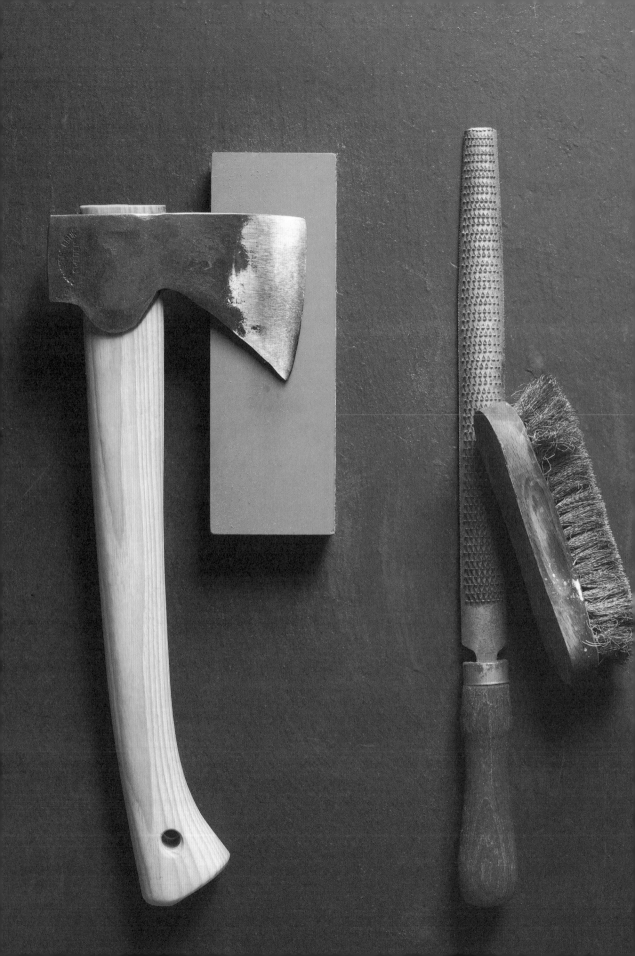

as in splitting firewood, causes splits that can be a very efficient way of removing waste when controlled. Blade work takes great skill to learn how to do properly. It requires a practical understanding of wood grain as well as tool choice and maintenance. Learning how to sharpen a knife or gouge is an art unto itself and crucial to blade use. Without a polished, razor edge, the blade approach will, at best, end in frustration.

Abrasives are a bit more crude and primal than blades. They rely on a ripping or tearing action to remove wood. An ever-increasing refinement of scratches is needed to achieve a smooth surface. They tend to be less concerned with grain direction than blades, although some understanding of grain helps. In some instances, work against the grain may be impossible due to sheer resistance. Cross-grain work rips through the short aspect of wood fibers quickly, allowing shaping and stock removal but leaving a rough surface. And work with the grain tears at the length of the wood fibers, which smoothes and refines shapes but ultimately is also the most labor intensive. A successful abrasive approach must be thorough if anything and requires an understanding of various "teeth" or file "sets," graduated grit abrasives, and a lot of elbow grease.

Blades and abrasives are not mutually exclusive. Nothing bad will happen if you decide to use sandpaper to smooth out a carving. Many people employ a combination of both approaches in their process. In fact, I advocate using the most efficient tool or technique to achieve a desired shape or surface instead of strict adherence to either tradition or convention. It goes without saying that if you want a knife or scraped finish, don't use sandpaper in the end, but if you are just trying to achieve a smooth surface, there are many other options. Likewise, using an ax to rough out a piece of wood prior to shaping with a rasp can save a lot of time.

The main thing to consider is that blades and abrasives describe two different carving tool families, which both work and are maintained differently. For instance, I may use three different types of files (coarse, medium, and fine), which I keep clear of clogging with a soft wire brush, to smooth a spoon made of ebony. Or I might use an ax and two different-shaped knives that I have honed and polished with a razor strop to work on a serving spoon made from a maple branch. In the end, whichever type of tool you are using, it is certainly the intention behind it that will make all the difference. The whole point of practicing is to be able to think less about the tool itself and focus more on the shape that you are making.

CLAMPING

One way to reduce the number of things to think about is to clamp your work to some sturdy object if you are able. Clamping helps immobilize the piece, allowing the focus of your force to be directed exclusively behind the carving tool and not in trying to resist your own cut. A simple screw-type clamp works just fine to secure material to your work table.

Not all projects need to be clamped in a vise, but you do need to figure out a safe way to hold any carving project that you are working on. You need both hands to use a mallet and a gouge at the same time, and you will find that it is much easier to clamp work that you wish to saw.

One very useful, old version of a work-holding device specific to wood-carving is what is known as a *shaving*

CLAMPS (left to right): Shaving horse clamp. Bench vise with wood plates. *(Opposite):* Screw-type clamp with piece of scrap wood used to brace.

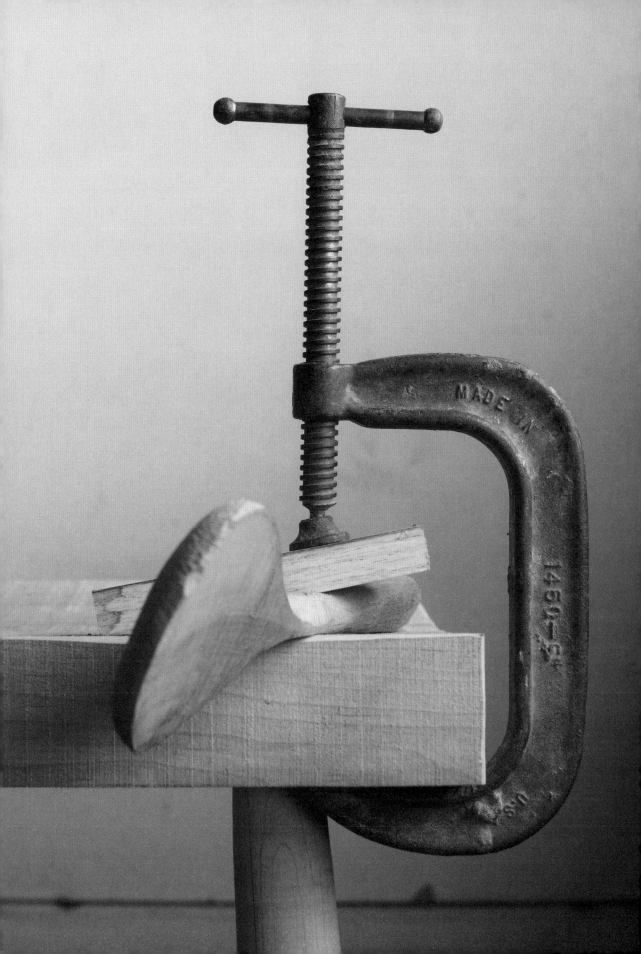

horse. This type of device uses a foot-operated lever to clamp the piece between some type of clamping head and a work surface. A shaving horse also, as the name suggests, provides the craftsperson a place to sit while at work. The device itself is also easily moved, making it a very versatile carving-work companion. Another great advantage to this type of clamp is that it is deceptively strong and quickly repositionable. This makes it well suited for resisting the pulling force exerted in carving techniques such as work with the draw knife or spoke shave. There are many different styles and traditions of horses. The really great thing about a shaving horse is that it is a simple, straightforward piece of equipment that is relatively easy to make yourself.

Work-holding vises of all sorts are now widely available and an indispensable part of any shop bench. The original style of vise for woodworking benches consisted of an all-wood screw and jaw mechanism built as part of a workbench itself. Wood components of vises are much more "edge friendly" than metal ones, meaning that they are less likely to damage the sharp cutting edges of

CLAMPS (left to right): *Bench vise with wood plates. Hand as clamp.*

chisels or the teeth of rasps with an errant cut or slip of the wrist. Cast metal components make up the bulk of most bench vises available today, but modern wood equivalents of bench vises do exist, and many people make their own. In comparison to iron, wood is quite soft and can be crushed by iron when sufficient force is exerted upon it. So outfitting metal jaws with wood plates helps protect carving tools, as well as the workpiece.

Our hands should be thought of as the clamps, or work-holding devices, when we carve with the knife. Knife work has evolved to utilize the opposite hand as more than just a static tool. Various cutting and slicing techniques take advantage of levering against your fingers, or pulling against the direction of a cut, both hands working in tandem, together but in the opposite direction, describing a scissorlike action that doubles the amount of force put into a cut.

Whatever the device or project, it will not take long for you to become aware of the need to clamp. How you are holding work is worth a great deal of consideration and practice. It can mean the difference between success or failure, conviction or fatigue and is an important part of getting set up to work both safely and efficiently.

SHARPENING

Using properly maintained, sharp tools is my number-one safety tip, but it is also my number-one process tip. It is very difficult to work with tools with dull or nicked edges and harder still to try to learn what you are doing if the tools react as if they have minds of their own. Trying to use damaged blades to carve is like trying to run a plow through the piece of wood. Thus, sharpening is a very important part of carving.

What use is a knife if you can't sharpen it? How long will it last? Or how about the gouge that is now at the bottom of your tool chest? These kinds of carving tools should not be thought of as disposable, or as in need of replacement if they become dull. If you learn how to sharpen and make it part of your process, some of these hand tools may well outlast you.

Sharpening edges is not easy. Fundamentally it is very simple in concept; nevertheless, some people can spend their whole lives attempting

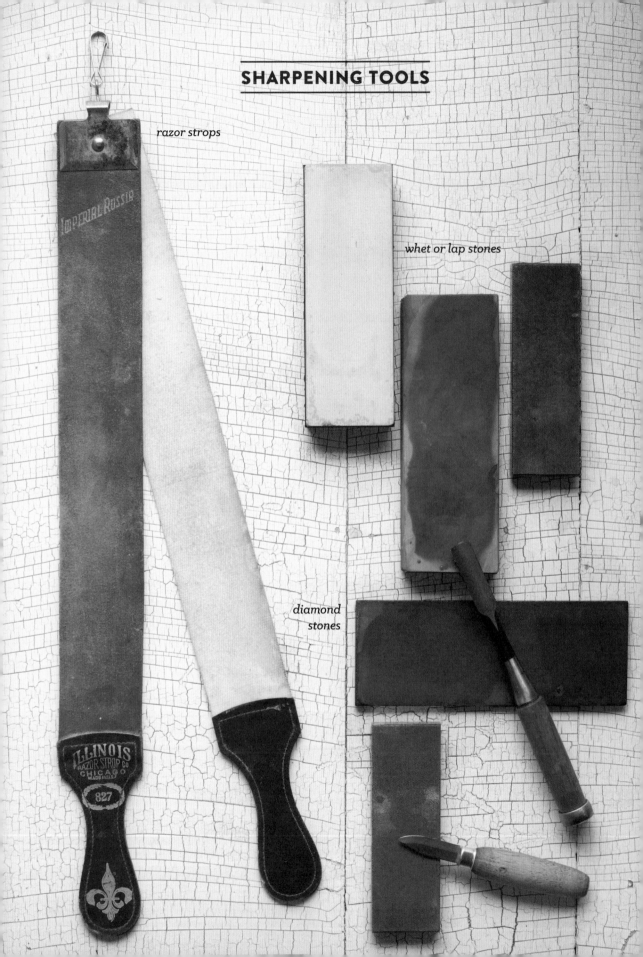

SHARPENING TOOLS

razor strops

whet or lap stones

diamond stones

IMPERIAL RUSSIA

ILLINOIS
RAZOR STROP CO
CHICAGO
MADE IN U.S.A.
827

and never quite getting it right. Sharpening could be the subject of its own book, but here is the basic principle: Sharpening is an abrasive technique that coverts gross to fine. For carving purposes, I'm going to divide it into three distinct stages: grinding, honing, and polishing.

Even though we think of steel as very hard and strong, some stones and minerals are harder still. These stones can be used to abrade the surfaces of a steel tool, refine them, and shape their intersection into a very fine edge. As you can imagine, the shape and quality of these stones has a great deal to do with the edges that they can produce.

Sharpening stones come in all different shapes, mediums, sizes, and grits. There are oil-lubricated stones, water-lubricated stones, natural, synthetic, diamond, and more. They come attached to machines and grinding wheels as well as in simple, small, flat slabs and conical chunks known as *whet* or *lap stones*. Beyond shapes, "grit" is used to describe a graduation of abrasive quality. The lower the number, the coarser an abrasive, and the higher the number, the finer.

POLISHING (left to right): *Buffing wheel with sharpening compounds. Sharpened and polished tools.*

Heavy grinding is rarely necessary if you take good care of your tools. Try not to drop them. Don't just throw your blades into a drawer or toolbox. Try to pick the right tool for the job every time. Occasionally, tips will break, tools will fall, and nicks will happen. Grinding should be reserved for only the most damaged of edges. Aggressive, heavy-grit stones can be used to reshape the tip of a knife or straighten the edge of a chisel. You might be picturing the quintessential pedal-driven, wheel-type grindstone. Modern equivalents exist both as handheld and bench-mounted electric versions, but for most carvers a coarse diamond whetstone is more than sufficient for all their grinding needs. Diamond stones come in coarse, medium, and fine grits; they are usually lubricated with water, and they last a very long time.

Honing is the process of flattening or truing a ground surface. Grinding leaves visible scratches on the cutting edge. Honing should remove these and produce a visibly uniform surface right out to the edge. I suggest 1,000- to 4,000-grit stones for this. I use water-lubricated stones (my personal preference).

After the blade's surface is "trued," I finish the honing process by pulling the tool away from the cutting edge, effectively "pulling out" a razor edge rather than trying to push the blade into becoming one. If all goes well, a very thin, near-microscopic "wire edge" will develop with these backward strokes. You should be able to feel this curl of steel with a light brush of your thumb against the blade's edge. Visually, it may be very hard to see this wire edge, but careful inspection in good light will show that it reflects light differently than your blade's edge (because it is on a different plane). You will be able to see this difference in its reflection, which should be uniform and inclusive of the whole blade, right out to the tip. Well-honed edges are capable of becoming razor sharp; that is, sharp enough to shave hair with. Carving tools should be even sharper.

FINISHING THE HONING PROCESS: *Backhand strokes sweep the knife out and away from the razor strop.*

Polishing is pointless without a well-honed edge. Once a blade develops a good consistent wire edge with a 4,000-grit lap stone and the surface and edge of the tool look uniform, it is ready for polishing. *Razor strops* are a good example of polishing equipment, but in truth, almost any flat, inherently nonabrasive surface will do. What is really doing the work is an added abrasive polishing compound that is imbedded in the surface. Thick fabric like that of a cotton canvas belt is perfect for holding abrasive compound, but a board or wooden dowel can also be charged with compound.

Today, grinding wheels made of felt are available in various hardnesses for electric machines that are made for polishing metals. Charging strops, belts, or wheels simply consists of rubbing them with compound. Compounds are available in various grits that generally come packaged as small cakes or sticks. Different colors denote different abrasive grits. Traditionally, Jewelers Rouge and Brown Tripoli make up the finer end of the polishing compounds. I prefer to use coarser grit compounds such as White

Diamond for polishing carving tools and spend less time at this stage of sharpening. Presumably the tool was already razor sharp.

With a charged strop, preferably on a flat surface, I polish my tools with the same action as in the end of the honing process, away from the edge, backward cutting motion, keeping the blade as flat as possible, and no flourishes of the wrist or little sweeping gestures at the end. Too much showmanship is more likely to round the edge over than to refine and strengthen it. Smooth, consistent, backward, flat, and balanced strokes, one for one side and one for the other side, are the key.

Finishing the polish on a piece of clean leather in the same stropping manner is the time-tested method for completing the sharpening process. The leather cleans and burnishes the cutting edge. This last step removes any microedge material that may remain connected to the edge, exposing what should be a very fine, consistent steel cutting edge. A well-polished tool has a strong, long-lasting edge and mirrorlike quality to it that is undeniable. Learning how to achieve this edge is worth the frustration that you may encounter along the way.

As far as application of all the sharpening techniques: Strop often to "freshen up" a blade, rehone if a problem develops (such as scratch marks within your cut), and grind only when absolutely necessary (such as when your knife has no tip).

So what do you really need for sharpening? For carving tools, whetstones and strops are sufficient and, for the novice, a great place to start. Machines for sharpening are expensive and initially unnecessary. First, it is important to learn to see what is happening to the edge that you are working on. Whetstones don't take up a tremendous amount of space, and although they may seem expensive for what they are, they are in fact invaluable when it comes to keeping your tools usable. Think about a whetstone as a necessary investment to make when you buy your hand tools, not after your tools get dull.

You will soon learn that it is far easier to dull a blade than it is to sharpen one. When sharpening, it is important to learn to use a consistent, isolated, and repetitive motion. I try to become more aware of my body movements, how my wrist rotates, and how my elbow hinges. And it is far more productive to proceed slowly and consistently—coarse, medium, fine, extra fine—than with reckless abandon when it comes to sharpening. I try to remember that a razor edge is produced not by brute force, but by balance and precision.

Beginning with whetstones will help you develop a healthy respect for how to generate cutting edges and the importance of good-quality steel. Without exception, higher-quality steel tools hold their working edges longer and thus require less sharpening and polishing. Grinding, honing, and polishing are all very labor intensive. It can take a long time to prepare an edge by hand; it is steel, after all.

ROTARY CARVING

I'm including a section on rotary tools because they are an extremely useful modern adaptation to carving of all sorts and seem to be largely overlooked. Most woodworking catalogs have a small segment dedicated to carving burrs, and recently a plethora of handheld electric rotary devices

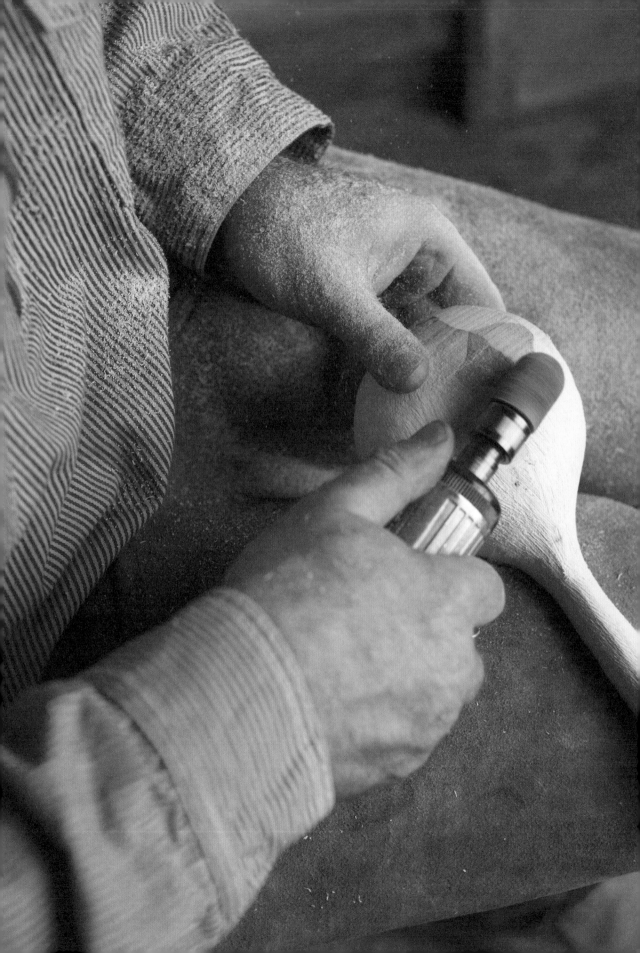

(along with a veritable library of burrs, bits, and attachments) have come to market. Bits, burrs, and heads generally come in either ⅛-in (3-mm) or ¼-in (6-mm) shafts. Shaft size will depend on the particular device's capabilities. These shafts are held in the tool by means of a wedge shape collet and a compression fitting.

I use pneumatic-powered die grinders when I am in the shop, but the basic principle of rotary carving is the same regardless of how the device is powered. The rotary device holds and spins these small bits and burrs, which do all the stock removal. Bits and burrs are interchangeable. They are manufactured in various profiles or silhouettes, which describe the shape of the cut that they will make. A spherical-shaped burr with a rounded profile will produce a concave cut. A cylindrical-shaped burr with a rectangular profile will produce a square cut. They work in much the same manner as a router bit or a drill bit, by spinning very fast and cutting or abrading hundreds to thousands of times a minute. Rotary carving seems to be more an invention of the metal-casting trades than the woodworking trades. Originally these rotary devices were

developed as an analog to the linear file, but because of their versatility they have been adapted to several industries and have a variety of uses.

For our woodwork, I will loosely divide the interchangeable inserts or bits into two basic categories to help you understand what you might be getting into when making a selection: file type and abrasive type. (I am categorizing them this way mostly to relate how each type responds to wood grain, not to imply that these delineations are an industry standard.) I classify most available carving burrs, which are typically made of very hard carbide steel and are characterized by helical cutting edges, as "file" type. These cutting edges look like the crisscross *set* pattern, the angle and geometry of file "teeth," but are very sharp. These burrs, as they are widely known, can leave a very smooth surface in wood as well as soft metals. Many of us are more familiar with this type of carving than we might like to admit, as most dentists use a very small-scale version of these types of carving bits to do their cavity and filling work. There are some insert blade-type, rotary carving heads, of a spherical profile, designed specifically for

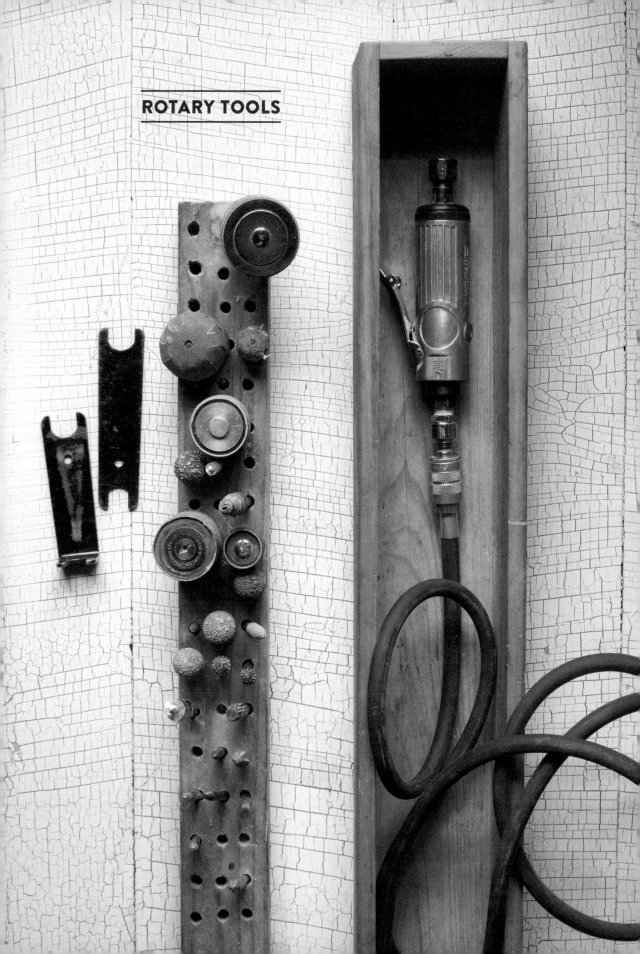

ROTARY TOOLS

woodwork, available today. These kinds of carving heads have replaceable blades to help keep a sharp cutting edge at your disposal. Largely, carbide burrs can be sharpened properly only by a professional sharpening service. They last quite a while and are fairly inexpensive.

I classify abrasive burrs as anything that accepts a sanding sleeve or is characterized by a rough, rasplike surface. There are drum-type sleeves, dome-type sleeves, and a variety of rasp profiles made of tungsten carbide that all fit this description. They leave the work surface abraded and rough, as the name suggests, and must be employed in a graduated way, as with other abrasive processes (such as sanding), and used in succession: coarse, medium, and fine.

The main difference between the file and abrasive types as it pertains to our spoons work is how each type reacts to the grain of the wood. Bits of either sort will burn if they are applied to the wood while spinning too fast. At running speeds suitable for woodwork, each type reacts differently to the direction in which it is presented to the wood grain. File-type bits are more aggressive; they will grab grain

ROTARY BURR HEADS (left to right): *Carbide file-type burr and abrasive rasp. Inflatable drum-sander abrasive.*

when cutting in the wrong direction, splinter the surface, and literally drive themselves around the work-piece. Abrasives can maneuver around changes in grain without as much grabbing, are a bit slower in stock removal, and leave a more abraded surface, but are also friend-lier, in this aspect, to use.

Rotary carving creates dust, so it is a good idea to prepare for this before you start. Even the blade-type burrs create very small chips, and a lot of them rather quickly. And with abrasives in general, it is a good habit to try to catch dust as close to the source as possible. Some shops have elaborate dust-collection systems, but for the kind of dust created doing spoons work, a shop vacuum is more than sufficient. I suggest organizing your rotary work in a nice sunny spot around the end of a vacuum hose.

This type of carving requires a few more tools to set up, you find yourself inextricably tethered to a power source, and the dust has to be dealt with, but it is a relatively safe, efficient way to remove wood, which is incredibly versatile and easy to learn to control.

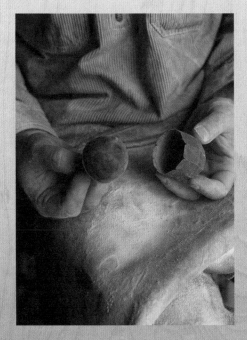 

ROTARY BURR HEADS (left to right): *Abrasive dome sanding sleeve. Rotary work with vacuum.*

SAFETY

Accidents happen. That is the nature of an accident. Tool safety is the consistent practice of maintenance, prevention, and learning where not to be.

Many years ago, tool safety and accident prevention was described to me in a way that has not only stuck with me but also served me very well. The principle is that two things need to go wrong at the same time for you to get injured. For instance, perhaps you are making a dangerous cut (the first wrong thing) and you are in a hurry (the second). This completes the recipe for disaster.

The fact is that we don't always work 100 percent safely, but we should try to have control over our environment whenever we do work. By the same token, just because an accident happens doesn't also mean that you will get hurt. Remove the variables. I might slip and fall while I am carrying my knife, but that doesn't mean that I will get cut, if I am carrying my knife in a safe way. A small measure of prevention goes a long way toward the bigger goal

of safety. The "two strike" principle helps point out that there are many variables involved in accidents and, thankfully, just as many ways we can make our practice safer and reduce the chance of injury.

In the shop and around heavy pieces of wood, proper attire is always a good idea, including a dust mask when sanding, a heavy apron, safety glasses, and no open-toe shoes. I am, however, a greater advocate of simply paying attention, and if any of these things become an annoying distraction, none are so necessary to spoon carving as your comfort and well-being.

The best tools for spoon carving are your hands—well, your heart first, your brain, and then your hands. Take care of your hands. Chances are your fingers will be the things most likely to get nicked while carving spoons. Controlling your knife prevents slipping, which is dangerous. Before you commit to a cut, think about where the knife or gouge will end up. Make sure that no part of your body is there! There are many safe cutting techniques and holds to practice. After a while, you will be able to sense if you are about to do something the wrong way. Nicks happen, but cuts are serious. Every time I have cut myself, I saw it happen in my mind's eye the moment before and knew that I was about to make a mistake. And in those cases I was probably not listening to my internal warning system because I was in too big of a hurry. (In fact, I had been accident-free for some time until we shot the photos for this book, which, I think, is a great example of why you should not try to carve if you are too distracted.)

Overall, for carving safety, remember to keep your tools sharp, don't rush your work, think about what you are doing, and try to concentrate on only one or two things at a time.

SELF-CRITIQUE

Critique is an important way to test ideas and better employ the experience that you have gained. Where you went wrong and where things went right. What part was easy and where you are having difficulty. Often, I find that there is a close relationship between an object being visually agreeable and functional. Smooth, clean lines and well-resolved, consistent surfaces indicate balance. Being critical of all these things is important. Use your eyes to see what you are doing. Watch the progress of your cuts. Look intently at your work to judge the accuracy of your lines. These are all ways to self-critique, but also remember to use your fingers. The tips of your fingers can serve as very sensitive calipers to gauge thickness that you can't see. They are able to judge depth and relative dimensions to an amazing degree of accuracy, and they can feel roughness that may not be visible.

One of the best ways to understand functionality is of course to use the object. Don't just imagine how a spoon will perform, use it! If you question how strong a spoon will be, break a few. We all have failed attempts; don't just throw them to the scrap pile . . . put them in the dishwasher to see what will happen.

What do we mean when we say wood finishing? Are we talking about sanding, polishing, or applying some magical liquid that makes wood impervious to everything? How do wood surfaces get smooth but remain tactile? How do we treat things made of wood so that they can be maintained and resist wear yet retain their organic presence? Spoon finishing boils down to one thing: to be able to wash the wood off after you use it, cleaning it as you would other kitchen utensils with regular old soap and water. Finishing wood can help it deal with the cycles of wet and dry, of the expanding and contracting that happens with washing. Unlike other wood items, spoons demand this working-type finish; that is to say, a surface treatment that can be maintained and resist wear. In part we are talking about sanding and polishing, but the truth is that any good wood "finish" begins long before you ever reach for a brush or rag.

TEMPERING AND CURING

The main consideration prior to finishing is that the piece must be dry. Wood that has been carved dry to begin with can begin the finishing process as soon as the shaping is done, but wood that has been carved wet, on the other hand, needs to dry. A slow, even drying process will minimize the likelihood that any cracks will develop within the piece. This can be accomplished by simply wrapping the spoon in kraft or other porous paper and waiting for everything to dry out, which might take weeks. Or it can be as simple as boiling.

Before putting green wood utensils to use, they should be tempered, cured, and oiled. Tempering is achieved by boiling the utensil in clean water. The extreme heat helps break down any latent tension that was in the original piece of wood, sterilizes the utensil, and actually helps extract locked-in moisture, allowing the wood to dry faster. I suggest 30 minutes of boiling for every ½ in (12 mm) of wood thickness. As most spoons are considerably thinner than this, they may take only 10 minutes or so to temper.

After the boiling process is complete, I remove the spoon from the pot, wrap it in kraft paper or a brown paper bag, and put it under my bench to dry. This curing step slightly slows down the drying process and keeps the wood from drying out too rapidly, which may cause cracks to occur.

A dry spoon is noticeably harder and lighter in weight than the green wood that you started with. Checking the weight is a good method to more precisely track moisture loss, but is hardly necessary. At any rate, for small spoons, this drying period rarely lasts for more than a few days. Humid weather conditions and some woods may lengthen the drying period. Often, the next day after tempering, a spoon is noticeably drier and ready to be finished.

All good finishing practices start with even better surface preparation. It is not uncommon to give a spoon a final light sanding or last scrape prior to the final finishing steps. Sanding is an abrasive technique that refines a surface by making ever finer scratches. One grit replaces the scratches of the previous grit, and so on. Very fine sandpapers are available that are capable of producing a fine polish.

Scraping is the blade-style equivalent to sanding. In essence, the edge of a flat piece of hard steel is worked into a very small burr by means of a burnisher. This small hook is used to shave very fine amounts of wood from the surface, in effect cutting wood fibers rather than tearing or scratching

TEMPERING: Spoons are boiled in clean water and given a light sanding post-tempering.

FINISHING TOOLS

finishing oils

tempering pot

soft-bristle brush

fine sandpapers

beeswax

them. In some applications, scraping is a much more efficient option than sanding, but it does require an understanding of how to create a sharp scraper edge and some skill, insofar as proper use. In the end, whether sanding or scraping, you should be able to caress the work with your hand and find no exception with what you feel, nothing that you want to change.

The finishing process can accentuate the color and grain of wood, and it can make a good-looking spoon great, but it should never be thought of as a way to take care of mistakes. Kicking issues down the path of your process is bad practice. A beautifully made piece will finish well; a poorly prepared one will not. Again, looks are only a small part of why we finish woodwork.

There are many different types of wood finishes, but not all of them are suitable for the demands of kitchen items. Verathanes, urethanes, and polyesters are out, which is a personal choice. Why would you want to cover a beautiful piece of wood with a layer of plastic, and then eat that plastic when it begins to wear off? I am an advocate of oil finishes on wood that will be used in the kitchen and needs to stand up to heavy use. Oil penetrates into the fibers of the wood, where it helps the wood resist absorption. Oil finishes are semi-permeable, meaning that while they are absorption-resistant, they also allow the wood to breathe, which is much better for the longevity of the wood and the finish as well. Oil finishes are easy to apply, easy to maintain, and get better looking with age and use, which can't be said about all that many things in general. What is even better about oil is that there are several entirely nontoxic, food-safe options to choose from.

OILS

Not all oils are created alike. Many natural oils can turn rancid after exposure to air. Olive and corn oils should be avoided. They are said to sour wood utensils and should not be used or thought of as finishing oils.

Linseed (which is also known as flaxseed) and walnut oils are examples of oils that polymerize when exposed to air, which means they harden somewhat. These oils make great, lasting, all-natural wood finishes. They are food-safe and readily available in grocery stores. Aesthetically, these polymerizing oils are characterized by having a yellowish cast, a color that they then impart to wood. These

finishes can put up with a lot of use and abuse. They are easy to maintain with simple hand washing and successive coats of oil if necessary. It should be noted that people who have nut allergies may have adverse allergic reactions to spoons finished with nut oils, so be sure to disclose when these finishes are used.

Mineral oil is another commonly used finish for wood utensils. It is 100 percent neutral, it never goes bad, and it is safe for food contact surfaces, while also imparting the same resistant qualities of other oil finishes. Mineral oil is a petroleum by-product; it never really dries, and when used as a utensil finish, it needs maintenance. It is however, absolutely clear, colorless, and odorless, which isn't to say that it doesn't accentuate the natural color and grain of a piece of wood. Mineral-oiled wood looks wet with water, which is, as they say, "water white." Maintenance consists of additional coats of oil as needed. Over time you generally have to apply these coats less frequently.

Oil can be applied by submersion, brush, or rag. Whatever type of oil you are using, the application process is the same: Flood the surface, let the oil soak in, wipe off the excess, and let the piece dry. Recoat if necessary. It is that easy. A dry sand can happen after the finish has been allowed to dry and before you add the next coat. Wet sanding can be added to the process of an oil finish just after you flood the surface. This technique can be used to immediately polish any grain that may be raised during finishing. Oil lubricates the abrasive action of the sandpaper and prevents fine papers from becoming clogged with dust. I reserve wet sanding for only the finest of sanding grits: 400, 600, or 1,000.

A mineral oil finish never really dries, as mentioned, but if allowed to completely soak in overnight, it is rarely still sitting on the surface the morning after it was applied. In the end the wood should feel soft but not greasy to the touch. Recoat if the wood seems dry or if the finish appears patchy. Buff with a clean, dry cotton cloth.

Polymerizing oils tend to be more viscous than other oils and can be quite sticky as they are going through their drying process. They require the added patience of waiting for the oil to dry or set up, which is more commonly referred to as curing. This can take days, depending on the conditions. Polymerization is a complicated chemical process in which exposure to oxygen creates bonding or cross-linking between fatty acids in the oil. Heating the oil prior to application can help speed up the process, as can the heat generated by the friction involved in buffing, but patience is a key part of the process. Walk away; let the oil sit. Also, successive coats should be applied only after the previous one has had a chance to fully cure. Many thin coats that have plenty of exposure to the air are far better in this respect than one thick, gooey one. One coat of oil on dry wood is rarely ever enough to evenly cover the surface, but seldom are more than two or three coats necessary.

Beeswax and wax-based salves are also food-safe finishing options. Wax in general is a tenacious substance; it never dries and is capable of both covering and resisting most everything. Wax can even be applied over an oil finish, but I observe the rule that once you use wax, there is no going backward. Wax is incredibly hard to remove once it is applied, so make sure that you want a wax finish before you experiment with it on something important to you. A beautiful wax finish is something to behold. It can be applied easily with a soft, short bristle brush and buffed with a clean cotton cloth. Wax is also very sensitive to moisture and heat, so its application may be limited by these conditions. As far as a successful spoon finish, I would reserve wax for only the most special of measuring spoons or spoons made specifically for dry goods like sugar, flour, or coffee.

I try to spend some time outside every day, even if it is just a few minutes to look up at the sky. I find the air therapeutic, I love weather of all sorts, I marvel at the passing of clouds, and I gain inspiration through this connection with the natural world. Our surroundings are full of reoccurring shapes, symbiotic relationships, causes, effects, the pervasive give and take of life, and the natural movement of all things. An open mind can transform a short walk into a trove of ideas and an endless source of raw materials. Often, all the materials that you need to make a piece are close at hand and simply waiting to be discovered. The naturally occurring and distinguishing characteristics you see may suggest the form that your work will take. A subtle crook or bend in a limb or a knot that diverts a branch may become the exact shape of a handle or the scoop of a bowl. These distinctions suggest more than just the form that branch may be shaped into; they are clues about what is going on *inside* the branch, which is all about the grain.

Going with the grain, taking a walk, imagining what shapes and forces lie beneath bark, and taking clues from your environment are more than just things to do or a way to see. I think about these ideas as a way to learn to feel, empathize, and interact with my surroundings. I can't overstate the importance I place on the feeling that is inherent in craftwork. For me, it embodies at least two-thirds of the work that I do. Not only is it the development of tactile feeling and muscle memory but also navigating with and engaging my heart as a design tool. I rely on feelings as a qualifier and indicator, especially when there is no obvious answer. Also remember that everything takes time, there is no rush, and your work ought to be pleasurable in all aspects, including selecting the material that you want to use. It is worthwhile to find wood that is of good quality and inspires you.

Spoons are best made from closed-grain hardwoods. I love using fruitwoods, such as apple and cherry, which are mildly sweet smelling (as you might imagine), plentiful, and easy to work with. Hard sugar maple also makes beautiful, tremendously strong tools and is another of my favorites for the kitchen.

For this spoon we will be searching outside for green wood, ideally freshly cut or nearly so, but certainly not seasoned or dried out. Some of the techniques we will be exploring rely on the wood being wet. Perhaps you live by some woods, or maybe they are trimming trees in your local park. Local orchards are an excellent source for branches, especially for fruitwood. Maybe there is an arborist in the neighborhood who can be a source for you. Or you could even be on the lookout for fallen branches after storms. Certainly pruning your own trees can yield more material than you will know what to do with. Don't feel you need to stockpile a lot of trimmings. Chances are that you won't be able to use all of them before they dry out. There are always more branches around if you just look. Keep your eyes open for the right ones.

CHOOSING THE WOOD

Orchard trees are generally pruned every winter to keep them healthy, so there are always branches lying around at that time of year. Ask if there are fresh trimmings or make a trade. Branches that are up to a year old will work fine. With older cuts there is a good chance that they will be too dry and cracked for enjoyable carving. Just because a cut branch

has cracks, known as *checking,* on the end does not mean that it is dry all the way through. Saw off a few inches from the end of a piece and take a look to see if is still green, which means it will be free of checks, and perhaps noticeably wet.

Green wood is about as close to being a tree as wood can get. It is very easy to carve with few tools. The heavy moisture saturation makes the wood fibers supple and a joy to work with using all types of bladed tools.

BEGINNING WITH THE BRANCH

Branches can be split between knots along the grain, using axes or wedges, into naturally formed spoon *blanks,* and worked mostly with simple knives after that. Splitting the wood at this point, rather than cutting it, takes advantage of the inherent shape and character of the branch and establishes a much stronger blank, free of "short-grain" sections that may compromise

APPLE BRANCHES: *You may use branches like these, which came from an apple orchard near my home.*

the integrity of the finished spoon by making it structurally weaker—an example of going with the grain.

The very center of a tree or a branch is called the *pith*. This is more noticeable with branch material than boards or larger chunks of wood, but even these other pieces can contain pith wood if they were cut close to the center of the tree. Often this part is very recognizable as a spongy core and is the source of unbalanced tension and stresses in a board or blank. In a cross-section, the pith would be at the centermost growth ring.

Looking lengthwise at a blank, the pith often appears as a darker fissure near the middle that traces its way down the length of the grain. Most cracks radiate out from this point. Look for the pith and plan to get rid of it. The easiest way to avoid having the pith end up in a finished spoon is to lay out your work either above or below it.

Once the branch is split, make a series of fine cuts at about 45 degrees, perpendicular to the surface of the side that you want to use. Turn the branch around so you can cut the entire surface in this manner. These

BEGINNING WITH THE BRANCH (top to bottom): *Split between any knots, in the direction of the grain. The pith runs down the center of the branch. Making paring cuts.*

are depth cuts, which guide and help to more easily pare this middle wood back beyond the pith. Paring cuts are made at a very shallow angle and perpendicular to the depth cuts across the grain of the wood. Effectively, you are planing the branch from the sides by removing the center ¼ in (6 mm) or so down to the depth cuts. Watch your fingers at this stage: Change your grip on the branch to keep cuts away from your hand.

A great technique to tighten control of your ax work is to choke up on the handle so that you are holding the ax as close as you can get to the axhead. This allows for close work without having to swing the tool. In this way, the axhead can be pushed into a cut, which can be a very useful technique for tight spaces and paring cuts that need to be precise. Using this technique, the cutting edge is more closely connected to your hand as you work than it is at the end of a long ax handle.

WORKING THE BLANK (top to bottom):
The pith has been pared away. Sketching the spoon shape with chalk.

WORKING THE BLANK

Keep working until you can see that you have removed this center pith material. Paring this away also helps clean up the split surface so that you can more easily draw on it.

Now comes time to visualize, the time to superimpose the final shape

you want on the split branch that you have. I like to take the time to draw out the basic shape and rough volume of the spoon that I am going for prior to making any major cuts.

Ultimately, there are two basic components of a spoon: a bowl, or scoop, and a handle. Layout work does not necessarily have to be any more involved than delineating these two elements, identifying where one will start and the other will stop. Much of the refinement in the shape will happen as you work, and some is in fact determined by the tools you use. I suggest thinking rough and erring on the side of being large. In the end, you can always remove more wood, but you can't put any back!

The next step begins the rough cuts and the initial definition of the outside curves. It is important not to get too hung up on how things look at this stage. The point of the work is to rough out the shape as efficiently and definitively as possible by removing excess. For this spoon, we will mostly be using a very sharp ax for the rough-out work, although the saw will come in handy as well.

STOCK REMOVAL

It is possible to split away large chunks of wood, utilizing *stop cuts* to control where the splitting stops. Using a hand saw, make two such cuts on either side of the bowl, just to the width of the layout lines for the handle. This enables you to remove most of the excess from each side of the handle.

I place the blade of my ax along the line of the split that I want to create and then strike the back of it with a mallet instead of trying to hit this line by swinging the ax. This way I have far greater control of where the ax ends and the split that I want to create.

The green wood is easy to cut, so small repetitive slices made with the grain work to get the blank closer to the layout lines.

The curve at the end of the bowl and the rough shape of the handle are parts to make sure to rough out with the ax.

THE SPOON EMERGES

Project the curve of the spoon on the side of the blank after you have shaped the front and begin to pare material back to your drawing.

STOCK REMOVAL (top, left to right): *Making stop cuts with a handsaw. Making stop cuts with an ax.* **(Bottom):** *Careful use of the ax can do much to remove the stock.*

THE SPOON EMERGES (top to bottom): Marking the curve of the spoon from the side. Trimming the back of the handle.

When I am working on the handle, I am careful to leave extra material at the neck just behind the bowl. This is inherently a weak spot in the spoon and needs a little extra attention.

BEGINNING TO SHAPE THE SPOON

I like to imagine a structural spine that runs down the back. I can work up to it and accentuate it with the ax, but I find the ax a little heavy to use to refine it.

With a little practice, patience, and caution, ax work can be quite satisfying and an efficient way to rough out carvings. The spoon blank looks a little more like a spoon at this point, but there are limits to how far we can go with just the ax. The shape is still very rough and needs refinement. I like to give myself a central axis to accentuate the idea of the structural spine and to provide a bilateral reference to work around before I switch over to the knife work.

This idea of symmetry is interesting and somewhat important to be aware of when carving. I am not suggesting that you strive to make perfectly balanced symmetrical spoons. Some of the most provocative shapes have some kind of off-balance visual tension. The particulars of the shape are entirely up to you. The concept is important because this axis will describe how you will need to approach the cuts in order to work with the grain.

Most of us use a dominant hand to write or work with, and that fact means that when we are carving wood, a position that works well on one side of the shape needs to be reversed for the other. Imagine that you are carving the very end of the bowl of a spoon. If you are right-handed, your left hand is holding the spoon. You are making cuts along the right side of the bowl from the widest point out to the tip, going with the grain away from your body. Now imagine that you are going to make similar cuts on the left side of the bowl. You'll soon find that something doesn't feel right, something has to happen differently. You'll need to turn the spoon over, turn the knife over, or cut toward yourself to keep the cuts going with the grain. You'll need to reverse the orientation. You will notice that this situation will crop up again and again as you work. So cuts that work on the right side of the axis will, in essence, need to be reversed on the left. This is the concept of bilateral symmetry as it applies to carving.

There are a few knife work techniques that may help you in working

BEGINNING TO SHAPE THE SPOON (top to bottom): *Marking the center of the spine of the spoon. Marking the center of the front of the spoon.*

with the grain and the challenges that come with not being ambidextrous: power cuts, scissor cuts, thumb-assisted cuts, paring cuts, and stop cuts. Practice these holds and cuts; they make up the bulk of knife work.

FIVE KNIFE-WORK TECHNIQUES

Power cuts help to further define the rough shape. To make a power cut, while standing, firmly grip the knife in your cutting hand, lock your wrist, and use the full force of your upper body by straightening your arm directly through the cut. The motion is close to your body and in a downward direction with the grain of the wood. This is a very efficient, powerful technique used to remove large pieces.

Scissor cuts are made at chest level either sitting or standing. The cut begins with the knife laid on top of the workpiece and the cutting edge pointing away and slightly downward from your body. Looking down at your hands, the configuration of the knife and workpiece should be in an "x" or scissor shape. Your forearms should be parallel to the ground and your elbows pointed well to the sides.

Once the knife is engaged in the wood where you wish to begin the cut, the cut is accomplished by quickly drawing your elbows inward to your sides. This motion pulls the knife through the wood as much as it pulls the wood through the knife, both arms working together. If done properly, your forearms should remain close to your ribs throughout the cutting motion. This technique is great for carving large chips off of the end of a shape such as the tip of the bowl or end of the handle.

Thumb-assisted cuts are a technique that utilizes the opposite hand from your cutting hand to aid in making deep cuts by pushing on the back of the knife with just the thumb. The extra leverage and control that the thumb adds make more physically taxing cuts possible while reducing fatigue of the cutting hand. These cuts can be made sitting down, should be made with the grain, and can be used to complete most of the rest of the rough-out work.

Paring cuts are slicing cuts that are not meant to take off a lot of material but are used to refine rough shapes and surfaces. It is a fallacy that you should never cut toward

KNIFE-WORK TECHNIQUES (top, left to right): Power cut. Scissor cut. (Middle, left to right): Thumb cut. Paring cut. (Bottom, left to right): Stop cut, marks endpoint. Stop cut for removal. (Pages 106 and 107): More paring cuts. The knife points to the pitch, top view.

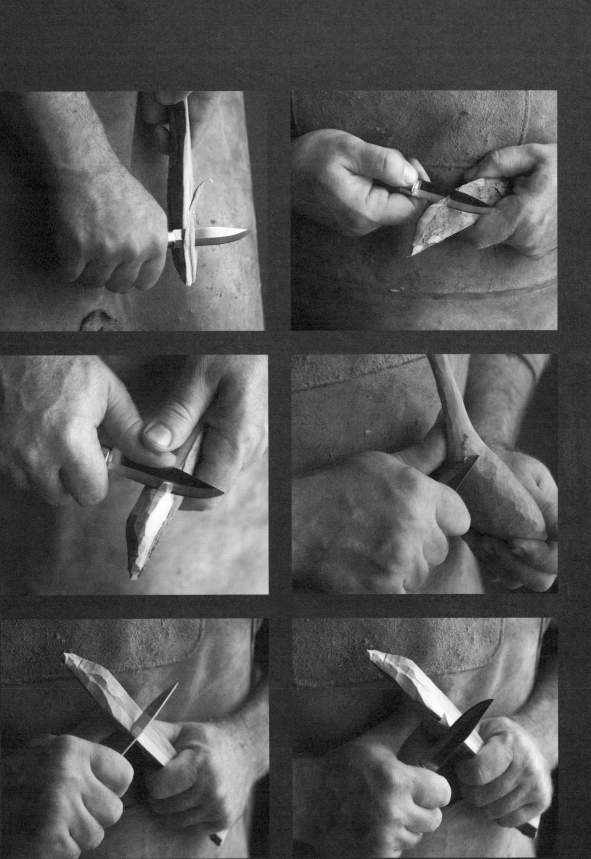

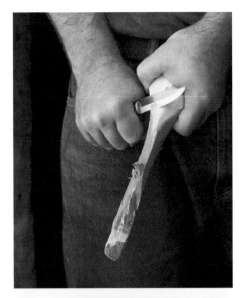

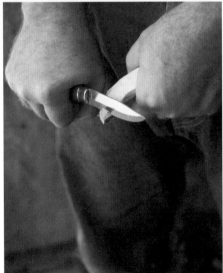

yourself. Often, it is completely necessary to make these types of cuts. The point is not to cut to a spot where your hands, fingers, knees, or thighs are in the way. Tucking your thumb behind the workpiece not only is a safe position to lever the knife against but also allows a lot of control over your knife work. Whether made toward yourself or away, these cuts are made at a very shallow angle to the wood.

Stop cuts are the combination of two cuts working together. Basically one cross-grain cut marks the cut's endpoint, and a subsequent slicing cut removes material up to that line. The cross-grain cut can be reinforced and more slices made to it, developing a distinct edge to work up to. A heavier version of this type of cut is possible by setting the limit cut by using a saw and then splitting the wood away with the ax up to that point.

DEVELOPING THE SHAPE

The refining process may feel a little like a juggling act as you repeatedly try to find the direction of the grain and stay with it.

Try to work down the slope of a developing curve; flip the spoon over

DEVELOPING THE SHAPE (top to bottom):
Cut downhill, with the grain. Use a stout knife to remove prominent corners and edges. Continue along the length of the handle.

if you need to. If you notice that a cut is grabbing the grain, stop and approach the cut from the opposite side. In practice, this quickly becomes evident when one direction cuts very smoothly, while the other tends to split or rip. A good rule of thumb is that you ought to be cutting downhill, or sloping downward, and with the grain, no matter what. Whether you are using a knife or a gouge, cutting downhill orients the work in such a way that the wood grain is supported by itself, and cuts happen smoothly and with control, rendering a predictable shape and a finished surface.

Of course there are exceptions to any rule, and knots and other dynamic grain may necessitate breaking the downhill maxim. The grain around knots may change direction. Knots represent a divergent branch from the one that you are working on. They can be beautiful but are notoriously troublesome and can be frustrating to work around. The best advice I can give you should you come across one in your work is to make small, shallow cuts and change the cutting direction as dictated by the wood. Generally the change in grain direction is quite localized and with a little care can become a nice natural feature to your carving, provided that it is in the right place.

I start the knife work with a large, stout knife that is good for making heavy cuts and begin by removing obvious corners and square edges.

SHAPING THE BOWL

With the general shape established and familiarity with the wood grain of the spoon now evident, I generally like to work a bit on defining the concave shape of the bowl. This is the point when the tools that you use become very specialized. A concave, inwardly curved surface requires a curved blade. For this spoon, I have chosen a gouge that can be manipulated both by hand pressure as well as by striking the end of the tool with a mallet to make heavier cuts.

If you think about the nature of a concave surface in wood and apply the concept of going with the grain, you might have the sense that the direction of the cutting motion is quite important. Fortunately, work on this kind of surface is predominantly made in a downhill fashion.

Gouge work to shape the bowl or the scoop should initially happen from the tip of the spoon down to the bottom of the developing bowl and then from the handle side to meet the front cuts at the bottom of the bowl.

The sides of the bowl will then be a bit rough but can be sheared smooth from the outside edges down to the bottom of the bowl. After the few large, deep cuts that I made by striking the gouge with a mallet, I now switch to cuts that I make just with hand pressure. Working in a radial fashion, from the developing edge down to the bottom, will keep you going with the grain and in a manner that develops the shape slowly and carefully. Green wood will yield to a sharp gouge quite easily, but if you find that this stage is difficult, make lighter cuts and just make more of them.

WORKING ON OUTSIDE CURVES

After the bowl is roughly shaped but looking good, I switch to a smaller knife that is a bit easier to control and go back to work on the outside curves.

With the concave areas roughed out, it is much easier to sense where to finish the outside. At this point I am making shallow paring cuts with the knife, removing facets from the previous rough-out work.

At this point, I think about and work toward the final form, perfecting the curve of the handle and the outside shape of the bowl. I feel the weight of the blank as it approaches becoming a spoon. I am increasingly

SHAPING THE BOWL (top to bottom): *A mallet may help in defining the concave part of the bowl. Gouging out the scoop of the bowl. Making many light cuts, working in a radial fashion to the bottom of the bowl.*

critical of shape as I imagine and practice with the functionality. I imagine eating with it or using it to serve. I hold the spoon less as if I am working on it and more as if I am using it, adjusting here and there with the paring cuts.

As the outside curves become more refined, I can finalize the inside curves using light paring cuts with the gouge, taking care to leave a smooth surface free of ripping, tearing, or roughness. Multiple light cuts made with the grain remove large facets and refine the concave aspect of the bowl. Carefully, I work the front edge of the bowl or the rim of the spoon and begin to refine the line where this change between the outside curves and the inside bowl begins.

FINISHING THE SPOON

I have chalked the rim to better see the edge as a shape and to control more closely the gouge work as I pare back the bowl. Too much gusto at this point may cut more deeply than you were planning. By nature, the shape that you are creating is delicate; misshaping it will compromise the strength of the spoon. The character and personality of the spoon lie in these transitions and the conviction of these shapes. More than just the

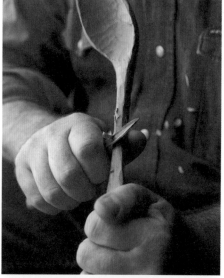

WORKING ON OUTSIDE CURVES (top to bottom): Making small knife cuts refines the outside of the bowl. Making shallow paring cuts to remove facets and smooth the handle. Working the handle back toward the bowl.

general refinement of form, the entire feeling and functionality of the spoon become evident in these moments, so I take extra care in finishing the gouge work.

With the inside of the bowl well defined and the lines established and smooth, the outside curves can now be finished, using the knife to make light paring cuts while taking great care to cut with the grain to smooth out all the surfaces.

If you tear the grain, or recognize that you have begun a cut in the wrong direction, stop and work in the opposite direction. Concentrate on making light, controlled cuts. This is the stage when the work comes to life. All the excess that was in the way is finally being removed and something noticeable happens: The stick of wood has been transformed into a spoon.

The lightest and perhaps most crucial of all the cuts are the edge cuts and any final, fussy work to be done on the transitions. These absolutely finalize the shape, sweeten the lines, and add to the functionality. They turn rough or even sharp edges into agreeable ones suitable for contact. Depending on the intended purpose of your spoon, not only might you

stir or serve with it but you may also use it for eating, so you want the entire surface to be pleasing.

Functionally, knife-cut wood fibers are smooth and polished just as they are. What your practice should focus on for knife-finished work is making continuous, interconnected smooth cuts, all made with the grain, over the entire surface.

Before putting green wood utensils to use, they should be tempered, cured or dried, and oiled. Tempering is as simple as boiling the utensil for several minutes in clean water. The extreme heat helps break down any latent tension and softens natural connective *lignin* that was in the original blank. Lignin is the organic polymer, or "glue" that holds cellulose wood fibers together. Boiling also sterilizes the utensil and actually helps the wood dry faster once the process is finished. I suggest 30 minutes of boiling for every ½ in (12 mm) of wood thickness. As most spoons are considerably thinner than this, they may take only 10 minutes or so to temper. After the boiling process is complete, wrap the spoon in kraft paper or put it in a brown paper bag to dry. This slows the drying process a little and

FINISHING THE SPOON (top, left to right): Chalking the rim to mark the edge of the bowl. Gouging to pare back the bowl. (Bottom, left to right): Making edge cuts around the bowl. Tempering spoons in clean, boiling water.

helps prevent the wood from drying out too rapidly, which may crack delicate parts.

A dry spoon is noticeably harder and lighter in weight than the green wood you started with. The drying period for small spoons rarely lasts for more than a few days. Humid weather conditions and some woods may lengthen the drying period. Often, the next day after tempering, the spoon is noticeably drier and can be ready to finish. Carefully monitoring the weight of a green piece is really the only surefire way to determine if it is dry. The wood will continue to lose weight as long as it is drying. When it reaches an equilibrium in moisture content, the weight will also stabilize. While weighing spoons definitively indicates dryness, it is a bit obsessive and largely unnecessary. Perhaps it is a good experiment to do once or twice, but in practice, just wait a few days, be patient, and see what happens. Applying a light coat of mineral oil after the spoon is dry will finish the carving project and prepare it for use.

In carving, knife-finished work is the sign of much patience and skill. Texturally, work that is finished "off the knife" is evocative of what is at the very essence of handmade: the human touch and the perfection of imperfection. As long as the final paring cuts went well and you are content with the final form, no further shaping or surface refinement is necessary after the spoon has dried.

If obsession prevails and you wish to do more shaping after the tempering and drying process, remember that the wood will seem much harder to work with. Detailed edge work and ornamentation may turn out cleaner when done after the spoon has dried, as the wood is able to hold a tighter edge. Also, scraping to smooth out small nicks may be more productive once the spoon is dry.

Before you carve your beautiful spoon into a toothpick, make yourself find a stopping point. I find knowing when to stop to be among the most difficult aspects of making things. The reality is that your work can always be better. If you are still unsatisfied at this point, you might find consolation in knowing that there are many more branches out there and more walks to take. Know that the next spoon will turn out better than the last and that there are always new tricks to learn and shapes to experiment with. Most important, remember that the fruits of our labors are much sweeter when shared.

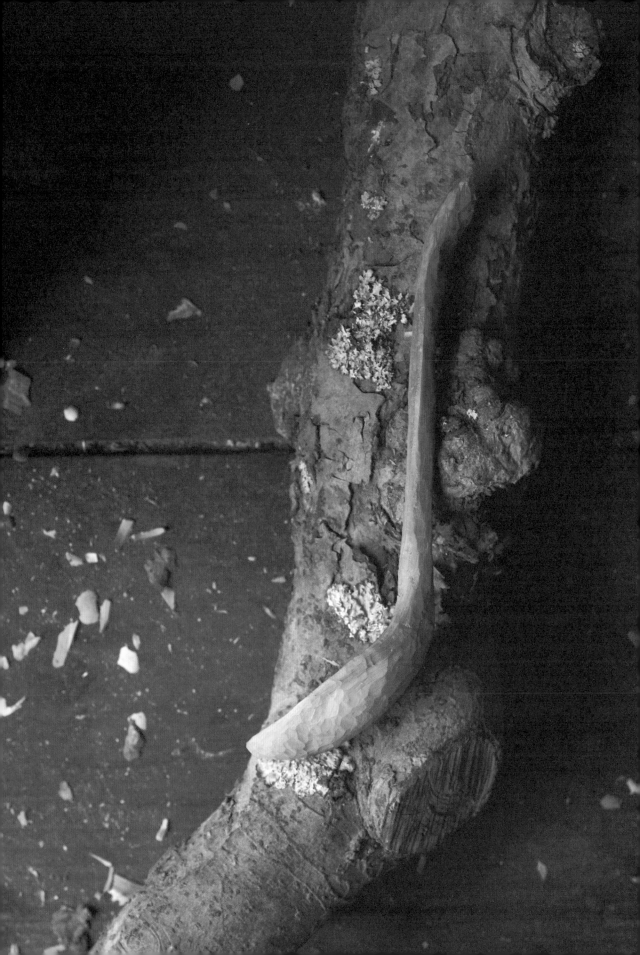

DESTRUCTION & CREATION,
MOVEMENT & BALANCE

We take for granted that making things is a creative process, but a more critical look at any creative process reveals a slightly bigger picture. It is a story about transformation, and half of that story is about destruction. We don't always think about it this way, but destruction is a necessary and integral part of creation.

Take anything, for example. Before it was what it is today, it was something else. That something else was changed somehow, it went through some sort of process, and that process was fueled by added energy. Somewhere along the way, it ceased to be that original thing, and it became something altogether different. The original was destroyed and something new was created.

For our spoons work, first our material was a tree, then it became wood, and then the wood was made into the spoon. Where once there was a branch, there is now a spoon. It seems obvious, but the reality of it is a bit overwhelming. In practice, it feels wrong to destroy a perfectly good branch when what you have set out to do is to create something beautiful. Exercising creativity is about reconciling the destructive beginnings of transformation.

―――――――――

There is a point in every creative endeavor I undertake when I reflect on the fact that what I have created is a mess, that everything is going wrong, and perhaps I have altogether ruined what I am working on. It happens in small ways, it happens in large ways, but it happens every time.

It is natural to have doubts. Our struggles with them tend to shape a great part of our lives. How we resolve our doubts speaks volumes about our process, our motivation, and our conviction.

What am I really worrying about along the way? That I am a failure?

That the spoon doesn't look right, or that the branch doesn't look like a spoon? That I have taken too much material off, or that I have lost the shape of the handle? So many concerns! What I am suggesting is that this moment of panic or heightened awareness is a fulcrum point, a change of perspective starting to happen during the transition from destruction to creation. Perhaps the moment of doubt is the indication that a shift is taking place. Maybe this "crisis" is pointing out the need to look at the material differently. If what I have indeed destroyed is the log, then I might just be on the right track to creating a spoon.

In trying to develop your own craft, self-reflection must be a good thing. Challenge can be a great motivator. I propose that doubt is a natural creative feeling to have; make the choice to let it be encouraging rather than discouraging. Remember, you are a failure only if you quit.

There is a larger and I believe more important connection to be made with the creative and destructive process, and that is to learn to see it as part of a continuum; your interaction with it is part of a much bigger balance. Are we responsible for the materials that we use, do we take too much, or can we replenish what we use? Both aspects—creation and destruction—must exist. Recognize the balance and try to pass it on.

We destroy so much already it seems important to me to imagine re-appropriating things for different uses, making do with, and taking care of what you have. Part of the creative spirit is about not only gathering inspiration from your larger natural environment but also learning to see things differently that already exist in your more immediate environment.

Firewood is generally available material. Initially, it is a heating fuel source, but it can also be thought of as a great source of precut hardwood logs that can be fairly easy to procure. Because it is often presplit, it is easier to read grain movement within a chunk of wood this size. Some of this material can be used to make beautiful spoons.

Logs should be hardwood, not softwood. Green or fresh split wood can be used, but often older material develops very interesting character. Large chunks of wood can retain moisture for quite some time. The biggest challenge in using this type of material is avoiding the cracks that develop as a log dries out from its ends inward. Inspect ends for *checks*, which are fissures that are the telltale signs of cracks within the wood. Checks begin to happen as wood fibers separate from one another perpendicular to the growth rings. They radiate out from the center of a cut section of log or branch, and look like fissures in the endgrain. Often the checks on the end of a piece of wood will describe the inherent splitting within. Larger, wider checks usually indicate cracks that originate deeper within the log than do the smaller checks, which may in fact disappear a short way into the log. Use these natural separations in the material to determine where your blank might be, as they almost always go with the grain and are an easy way to pare the log down to spoon size.

SPLITTING AND CHECKING WOOD

Wood splits more easily with a wedge than with an ax. The broader aspect of a wedge forces wood grain apart rather than trying to cut it. Even the most difficult of logs can generally be split using two wedges. One is driven in using a heavy hammer, which begins the split. If that is not sufficient, then the second wedge can be driven in farther along the split to apply even more force to the developing crack. The force of the second wedge releases the first wedge. If the log still hasn't split, then the first can be redriven even farther down the split, one wedge leapfrogging the next, and so on. Logs that are difficult to split, however, indicate that knots or other grain anomalies may be holding the log together, making it potentially unsuitable for carving blanks.

Once the log is split down to a more useable size, crosscuts will reveal the depth of the remaining checks. On close inspection, if these cuts reveal the blank to be check-free, then you can proceed with the

SPLITTING AND CHECKING WOOD (top to bottom): Splitting the piece of wood with a wedge and and mallet. Scanning the end for checking. Looking at crosscuts for checking.

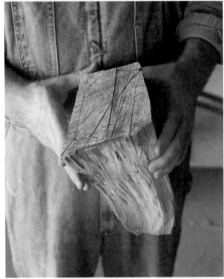

layout. If your end cut reveals that checks remain, make another end cut. Keep cutting until you find uncracked wood. In larger work these end checks are not the end of the world, but they may be catastrophic in a spoon, with delicate areas like the handle and the edge of the bowl, so keep searching. Generally speaking, if you have cut more than 3 to 4 in (7 to 10 cm) and are still finding major checks in your would-be blank, it may not be the piece of wood for you. Keep searching. It is worth finding the right piece before you put the next couple of hours of work into it.

Split wood is quite rough, so I clean up the surface with small leveling cuts of the ax. A more uniform surface is easier to draw on and work, plus I can begin to see underlying grain more clearly once the surface becomes smoother. This step is not necessary, and the surface need not be perfect, just clean enough to draw on.

ROUGHING OUT THE SPOON

I am a big believer in drawing as a design tool. I think that the more time you spend cultivating your ability to draw, the more you will be able to imagine, and the things you make will

ROUGHING OUT THE SPOON (top to bottom): Drawing the spoon on the blank. Removing stock along the handle with the handsaw. Removing stock around the head of the spoon with the handsaw.

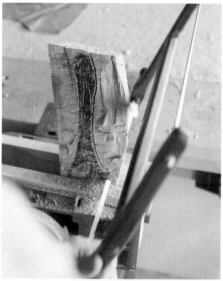

be closer to your vision. It is also far easier to erase and redraw a line than it is to split another blank, so draw, redraw, define, guess, erase, or level the surface again. All the time spent during layout is time well spent. Think about the drawing as the first gesture you make to the wood about the spoon. The first suggestion of what may be inside. I like to work back and forth, to develop the right curves, a little more here, a little less there. Now is the time to project ahead, see where knots may interfere or where they might be useful, avoid checks, and take advantage of the grain.

A saw is a very efficient way to remove a large chunk of stock very precisely. For carving, saws can save a lot of energy when it comes to roughing out a shape, but to successfully use the saw for this, your workpiece will need to be well secured. Simply standing on the blank will not do for this kind of technique. A vise or clamp is required.

I have mounted a pattern maker's style vise on my workbench. It operates on a basic screw principle, which tightens clockwise and loosens counterclockwise. The entire vise can also pivot from vertical to horizontal orientation and then spin 360 degrees. Once clamped, the position of a workpiece is adjustable in multiple axes by means of levers and cam-locking mechanisms. The adjustability of this vise minimizes the need to unclamp and reclamp many times as your work progresses. It is a nice way to hold work, but a much smaller and simpler vise would suffice for the saw work. Using a clamp to fix the blank to the end of a heavy table would work just as well.

As long as you have a very good idea of the waste that you want to remove and the ability to clamp your blank, using a saw to rough out a shape can save a lot of energy. Not all saws are created equal, and in fact there are saws that are specifically designed for cutting with the grain, saws that are designed to cut across the grain, saws that are designed to make only straight cuts, and ones that will cut curves. There are many variations, but the main factors are depth of blade to the teeth and number of teeth per given length of blade.

For cutting curves in small stock like spoon blanks, I find that a frame-style saw outfitted with a narrow blade that has many teeth works as well as any machine. I like to use Japanese-style saw blades, which are designed to be used on the pull stroke rather than the push. I find these to be incredibly sharp, accurate tools.

They may take a little getting used to, but with practice, these saws can become indispensable to all sorts of woodwork. The thin blade can trace all manner of curved lines, and the fact that it is also repositionable within the frame means that the frame can be adjusted to one side or the other should it begin to limit the cut or get in the way.

The frame saw is a great addition to any tool kit. An ax can be intimidating in that it takes strength to use for any length of time and it is inherently quite dangerous to use on small carving projects like spoons. Think about the efficiency and precision of the saw. All the cutting action is focused along a very thin edge.

BEGINNING THE THREE-DIMENSIONAL WORK

Orthographic projection is a way of thinking about an object as if it were projected onto a flat plane and we were able to view it from the cardinal points of front, side, and back views. Although this is an abstraction, the idea can be incredibly helpful in finding how a finished shape relates to a block of material. First we outline the

BEGINNING THE THREE-DIMENSIONAL WORK (top to bottom): *Sketching the side view. Sawing off rough cuts. The fully rough cut workpiece.*

finished piece from the front view as a drawing and cut along that shape. Then we project, by drawing, what the piece will be like from the side view and cut along that shape. In essence, by cutting out these two views, we have roughed out our form.

THE SPOON EMERGES

For spoons work, front-view and side-view projections are a great starting point. Rather than attempting to project an additional end, or top view, I just begin taking the corners off in a regular manner. Using my hand as a marking gauge, I fix a regular dimension in from the corner of my roughed shape and draw additional cut lines along its length. I use my hand as a relative marking tool like this quite often. I call it the "finger marking gauge." Fix the projection of your pencil or crayon between your thumb and index finger and then extend your middle finger to the edge of the workpiece as a guide. Think about this hand configuration as a unit or a dimension. Without releasing your grip, trace along the edge with your middle finger while drawing a line that is the fixed, projected dimension

THE SPOON EMERGES (top to bottom):
Finger marking. Cutting away the excess. Seeing the spoon form for the first time.

in from the edge. In this manner, a very regular line of equal depth can be drawn along the edge of a workpiece. The finger marking gauge technique works well for curved and straight surfaces. This layout line indicates the corners that can be "knocked off" of the spoon blank.

The thinner a piece becomes relative to the length of a saw blade, the easier it is to saw through. The less resistance the wood is able to provide per stroke, the easier a cut will be to make. The top view cut is the most difficult cut, followed by the side cuts and finally the corners, which are fairly easy to remove.

Even just removing the corners helps better reveal the shape within. Inspect your layout lines and be critical of your cuts. Try to remove any high points or remaining corners before you move on with the process of shaping the outside curves.

WORKING WITH RASPS

For as crude and rough as a rasp is, I find it to be a very satisfying tool to use. Hundreds of tiny teeth each remove one small bit of wood as the tool is pushed across the workpiece.

WORKING WITH RASPS (top to bottom): Using a rasp to shape the sketched form. Using a flat rasp to shape the curves. Using a barrel rasp on the outside curves.

Because of the set, or direction, of the teeth, a rasp is designed to work going in one direction, not unlike the saw or other file-type tools. So the focus of work when using the rasp is to cut on the push stroke only, even though the body motion is back and forth.

Working across the grain makes quick work of any corners that were left after the sawing operation, and you should be able to get a glimpse of the underlying curves rather quickly. I try to divide the outside curves' rough-out work between the back of the spoon and the front. Work around the form, using the rasp to cut down the curves and work off edges. In this way the large teeth of the rasp won't get hung up on the opposing wood grain or the rim of the bowl.

After a bit of initial rasp work around the back of the handle and the bowl to define the form, I draw a line down the "spine" of the spoon. This line is only a visual reference, but it does help me understand how much material I am removing and where it is coming from. It also begins to establish the anatomy of the spoon, the structure and attitude of the handle, and the apex of the back of the bowl.

Find a nice line and then continue to refine the volume of the back to it. Here, I continue to remove wood relative to the layout line, completing the rough shape and all the outside curves of the back.

Reposition the spoon in the clamp to work different ends. Try to find a position that allows you maximum access to the workpiece while also firmly securing the blank against the cuts you are making with the rasp. Work on the front of the spoon in a similar manner to the back.

Clean up the shape some and then outline the layout from tip to tail (this line should extend all the way around the spoon now). Use the line to judge and maintain the balance of the shape as you remove material where it is necessary. The outside curves should be well established at this point, the symmetry evident, and the spoon blank should already feel good to hold. If not, keep rasping.

FINISHING THE RASP WORK (top, left to right): *Drawing a line down the spine of the spoon to create a visual reference for balance. Rasping from each side to the spine midline.* **(Bottom, left to right):** *Workpiece in clamp, rasping the front side. Balancing the shape of the bowl (note the silhouette).*

CREATING THE INSIDE CURVES

Next is the layout work for the inside curves. Marking out the bowl delineates the balance between the inside shape and the outside shape by defining the side or wall thickness. A strong axis allows for easy placement of the ends of the bowl, and I use my finger marking gauge to project the sides about ¼ in (6 mm) in from the edge. This is a good dimension to shoot for at this rough-out stage. For the sake of visualization, I have darkened the whole layout shape to better show how to begin the carving work.

The spoon gouge is shaped to be able to scoop out small chunks, one chunk at a time. Its curved shape allows the cutting edge to generate deep recesses. I begin directly in the center with the grain, initially hitting the butt end of the gouge with a mallet to make each cut.

Opposing cuts will free chips at the bottom of the stroke. Gouge cuts at the cardinal points create a floral pattern that begins the hollowing-out process.

FINISHING

Radially, consecutive cuts widen the pattern into a hollow. Overlapping

CREATING THE INSIDE CURVES (top to bottom): Marking the bowl. Gouging out the bowl. Gouge cuts in floral pattern.

one round of cuts with the next removes high spots along the curve and eventually smooths the developing edge of the hollow. I work out to the layout lines, making sure that the deepest part of the hollow is also within my ¼-in (6-mm) wall rough-out dimension.

The outside curves and the inside curves are well established and roughed to a minimum thickness of ¼ in (6 mm). For all intents and purposes, at this point the blank has ceased to be a blank and become a roughed-out spoon, albeit a bit heavy.

The next stage of the process is to refine the outside curves and further smooth the surface left by the heavy rasp. I use finer-grade rasps and round files to do this work. In theory, if I have ¼ in (6 mm) of material left at this point, the outside curve refining process should take an additional ¹⁄₁₆ in (2 mm). None of these dimensions are absolutes. They are only guidelines, and with experience, no measuring will really be necessary. The main idea to focus on is that you should leave yourself enough material to be able to finish the spoon smoothly but not so much that you realize that there is still a lot of material that you

FINISHING (top to bottom): Making overlapping cuts to expand the bowl. The roughed-out bowl. Refining the outside curves with a fine, curved rasp.

want to remove at the final stages of the surface work.

WORKING THE EDGES

With outside shaping coming to an end, and the surface smooth, flowing, and free of heavy rasp marks, the focus begins to shift from the structure and surfaces of the spoon to the edges. How do these surfaces relate to each other? I am accentuating these lines to focus the work toward refining the edges. On the handle where the front and back meet, I am not trying to develop a sharp edge as much as generate a pleasing, consistent shape. I am easing the curve by adjusting the edge with the fine files. With the bowl, I am refining the wall thickness further by making light paring cuts with the spoon gouge, levering the tool from the very edge down to the bottom by hand, no mallet.

This will be the final inside curve surface with this spoon, so I take great care to make smooth cuts, smooth out rough cuts, and work the edge thickness down to about ⅛ in (3 mm). Wall thickness and depth can remain a bit thicker than this, but the very edge of the bowl can be worked to this

WORKING THE EDGES (top to bottom): Marking the rim of the bowl to provide a guide while refining. Smoothing out the inside of the bowl. Making final paring cuts to the bowl.

dimension fairly easily. Ultimately, I observe the spoon from an angle that allows me to perceive both the depth of the bowl and a good portion of the outside shape. I ask myself, do the two shapes respond to one another visually or do they appear discordant? Generally I can tell if the bowl doesn't look deep enough, because something will seem out of balance. At this stage I use my fingers as calipers, which are very sensitive to discerning relative thicknesses.

When no rough gouge marks remain and the bowl looks and feels good, I make four final paring cuts along the rim of the bowl to finish the shape. Starting at the apex I make a sweeping cut to the right and one to the left along the edge all the way to the middle, and two corresponding cuts from the very bottom of the bowl near the handle to meet the cuts from the top.

SANDING

Sanding is the next step. I try not to think about sanding as a sculptural step in which I am changing the shape, but more a finishing step for surface refinement. Initially, I rip sandpaper sheets into thirds. I like

SANDING (top to bottom): *Sanding with paper around dowel. Sanding with paper folded into thirds.*

to wrap the sandpaper around blocks of various shapes to give it more structure. I begin refining the surface with a piece of dowel wrapped with some coarse sandpaper. I use this in much the same way that I would use a file, except that the sandpaper will cut in all directions—back and forth and side to side. Fresh sandpaper always cuts the best, so make sure to use the whole piece, getting that initial bite out of each area of the paper.

Another way to use sandpaper is to take a smaller strip from a full sheet and fold it into thirds, grit to the outside. In this fashion, the folds create a neat pad in which the paper's own grit helps provide resistance that keeps the pad together as you sand. It also can be refolded when one side becomes too dull. Yes, sandpaper gets dull. Getting a fresh piece when the paper becomes dull is by far the most efficient way to sand.

Sanding is a labor of love. And it is very easy to get lost in it. The more complicated the shape, the easier it is to get lost. It is best to be as systematic and thorough as possible when sanding. I try to establish a sanding plan for a piece and stick to it so I know where to start and, more important, where to stop. Such plans are referred to as schedules. Here is what a sanding schedule might be like:

- Begin with coarse-grit paper. Sand the front completely. Sand the back completely. Pay special attention to the neck of the spoon, especially the transition between the handle and the bowl. Work right out to the edges but don't address them yet. Finish sanding with the grain. Do everything once again just to make sure all rasp marks are gone.

- Change to a medium-grit paper. Sand the front completely. Sand the back completely. Work right out to the edges but don't address them yet. Finish sanding with the grain. Go over everything once more.

- Change to a fine-grit paper. Work surfaces as before, being very thorough. Finish sanding with the grain, then address the edges as their own element.

- Change to a fresh sheet of fine-grit paper. After the extensive surface work, the shape of the edge should be a well defined line of no more than ⅛ in (3 mm). Reconciling how the inside and outside curves come together is all that is left. To do this, I bevel both inside and outside edges equally with the fine-grit sandpaper to meet each in the middle.

Sanding schedules vary in application. I use papers graded to 100 grit, 150 grit, and 220 grit for coarse, medium, and fine. The number matters less in practice than that the paper that you are using efficiently removes the previous tool or grit marks. Jumping too many steps will result in a lot of wasted energy and scratches that never seem to come out. Sanding reminds me a lot of cleaning or scrubbing surfaces. You really want to use the most efficient tool to get the job done.

ADDING DETAILS

After the fine sanding is done, I lay out any additional details. The shape is resolved and the surface is smooth

ADDING DETAILS (top to bottom): Drawing a hole on the handle. Drilling to start the hole. Carving out and finishing the hole.

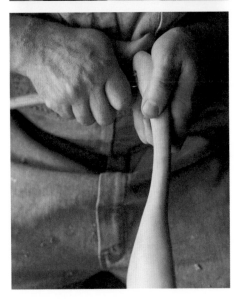

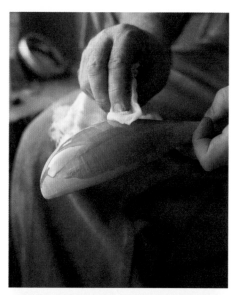

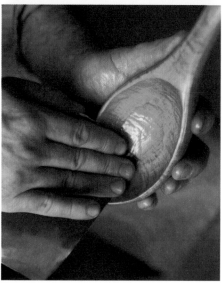

FINISHING WITH MINERAL OIL (top to bottom):
Applying the mineral oil with gauze. Wet sand-
ing with very fine sandpaper.

and it is easier to see what the next steps might be. For this slightly more complicated spoon, I incorporated a way to hang up the spoon. I projected an axis and then marked a hole to cut, trying to balance the negative and positive aspects of the hole. The edges should not be too thick nor the hole too big.

With the spoon back in the vise, I use a drill to begin removing material. Several carefully made holes of various sizes help make quick work of the rough-out step. I start with a small pilot hole of $\frac{1}{16}$ in (2 mm) to make sure that the hole is oriented properly front to back. I find a small bit easier to align and far more forgiving than a larger size. After I make the pilot hole, I widen it with successive drill bit sizes. Each successive size up can adjust the alignment, if necessary, until the hole has been drilled approximately to the layout line. Several holes drilled in this manner can remove a great deal of material prior to carving work.

I follow up with a very sharp, small blade carving knife. First I concentrate on removing the waste between the holes that I have drilled, then I begin to define the edge of the hole that I ultimately want. I make quick, sweeping cuts between 12 o'clock and 3 o'clock, 12 o'clock and 9 o'clock, 6 o'clock and 3 o'clock, and 6 o'clock and 9 o'clock.

I work the front of the spoon as well as the back to refine the edges of cuts around the hole. I am choosing to leave some knife-finish texture on this spoon. I think the inside surface finish of this hole and the inside curves of the bowl are smooth enough and beautifully evocative of the hand process, so I don't want to sand these any further. In general, before I consider oiling anything, I give it a once-over, a final round with the fine sandpaper to remove any finger-prints or oils that the wood may have picked up from being handled while I carved the hole.

FINISHING WITH MINERAL OIL

Mineral oil is a very easy-to-use finish that is also widely available. I like the fact that it is protective and accentuates the wood grain without changing the color too much, and it is easy to maintain as part of a regular cleaning schedule. I apply the oil with a piece of gauze or a clean cotton cloth, flooding the surface first.

With the surface saturated, I then wet-sand with a very fine sandpaper. This is to say I use the oil as a lubricant to polish the already finely sanded surface of the spoon. Wet sanding works best with papers that are designed to be used either wet or dry. The papers that look like the color of dark gray slate work quite well for this purpose. I use paper graded to 400 grit to wet-sand. After the oil has been allowed to soak into the wood, ideally 24 hours, additional sanding using 1000 grit and another lighter coat of oil may be added to the schedule to really polish the piece. This final step may not be deemed necessary for finishing the piece, but it will be how you take care of the spoon in the future, using a very, very fine abrasive and a light, nonsaturating coat of oil to maintain your spoon between washings.

Oiling is a dramatic step, so prepare yourself. Often it will reveal many hidden features of the wood that you have been working with. Some of those spots in the grain that were previously giving you trouble may turn out to be quite beautiful features in the finished piece. For example, the oil really brought out a quilted grain pattern along the back and handle of the spoon that I had not noted while I was working on it.

Who would have thought that such a beautiful spoon began as a chunk of firewood? I don't think that there are any set prescriptions for achieving perfect balance in a piece, effectively reconciling the process of creation and destruction. These words should instead be taken to describe an active process, not a prescribed plan. I think it's important to be sensitive to the push and pull between creation and destruction and to try to recognize that you yourself are an active part of a far larger economy and continuum of energy.

Efficiency is a big part of the equation. It is important to critique how much energy we spend and to what end is it applied. In many small ways we can refine our process, gain experience, and get better. But maybe it is even more important to consider where the energy that we use comes from and what we choose to do with it. Within the bigger picture, part of each of our responsibilities is to become the catalyst for change ourselves, and to become the vehicle for a larger creative energy.

The transformation between destruction and creation can mirror cycles within our lives. To become the energy that is needed to effect change, no matter how much we think it might take, and to become a conduit for this transformation is part of our human calling, part of our collective purpose, and ultimately a choice that we must make. Within this choice, and these cycles, however the scales are weighed, we must remind ourselves to endeavor to do good work . . . and remember to work for what is good.

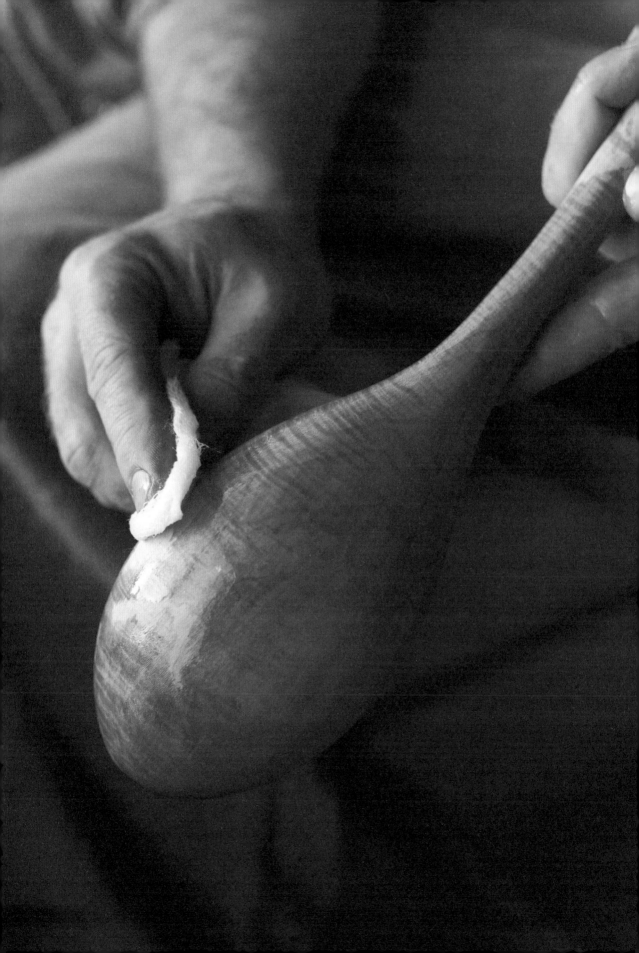

ADVANCED SPOON PROJECT:

INNOVATION & TRADITION

I find it interesting that in its time, the water wheel– and belt-driven workshop in the Shaker community of Hancock in southwestern Massachusetts was considered to be state of the art, whereas presently we might regard the facility as antiquated, poorly heated, and quaint. In their time, the Shakers were, among other things, great champions of innovation and technology.

Innovation by nature needs to be grounded. By definition, it is an addition or betterment made to some existing process. Rather than being separate entities, I believe that innovation and tradition go hand in hand. Each needs the other as a frame of reference, and hopefully they inspire one another in point and purpose. I would propose that for genuine progress to be made we must take both the past and future into consideration, and that our solutions are able to honor both in our efforts to move in the only way that we are given—forward.

Part of our carving practice needs to be concerned with efficiency. One of my favorite truisms for all sorts of labor is that "if it feels like you are working too hard, you probably are." Constantly questioning technique and tool use, learning what is a waste of time, and discovering where best to use our energy are all part of the learning process. Part of making things can certainly be therapeutic in practice. We make things for many reasons other than just money, and the processes and tools that you use or feel comfortable with may reflect decisions that have little to do with how quickly you can accomplish some operation. Some processes may themselves yield unique and desirable results, or perhaps they are limited by where you choose to do your work. The point is that no matter what process you are interested in, you should strive to do better, become more efficient, learn more, and of course share your results.

One of my favorite Shaker quotations comes from a letter by Thomas Damon to another furniture maker, George Wilcox, dated December 23, 1846, in which Thomas shares construction information about how to make a particular desk. At the end of the letter, after eloquently describing the concept and function of the piece, he admonishes George to suit himself as to the particulars of size and formation, closing with, "For where there is no law, there is no transgression."

Innovation without context can easily be lost. Tradition that is inflexible is ultimately doomed to wither rather than grow. Even tradition that is open and progressive in some ways may also find its limits in others (as the Shaker communities themselves eventually began to experience).

What truly transcends the moment? Often, it seems that it may be something completely unintended. Certainly the answers to these questions are not for us to know in the present, as they tend to be the sorts of things that play out over life-times or even longer.

STARTING THE SPOON

I had been saving this piece of holly wood for many years now. It was one of those rarities that sits on a shelf collecting dust, waiting. We have previously explored using branches and firewood to make spoons, so for this example I thought that using a particular piece of wood that was special to me might be a useful variation. This last spoon example seemed a fitting use for such a nice piece of beautiful wood.

Many lumber suppliers have bins of "shorts" that they are happy to get rid of. Small precious pieces can make great gifts for your woodcarving friends and can be purchased through most woodworking catalogues. Small billets of wood of all sorts and types are available from all around the world.

Sometimes when I'm in the shop, designing, trying to innovate, I will find an interesting piece of wood like this one and begin drawing directly on it, manufacturing my own inspiration, visualizing what could be inside, and opening up to the potential that I may discover something special. Chalk works well for me because it can be so gestural, so expressive. At spoon scale, drawing with chalk can be very intuitive. The lines are easy to balance, and it erases easily.

I cannot overstress the importance that I place on drawing as a design tool. Developing your ability to draw will help you describe your visions to not only others but also, even more important, yourself. No computer, no superfluous extra layer; just a pencil and a piece of paper or in this case a piece of chalk and a chunk of wood.

Drawings can be a great way to problem-solve at any scale, but for spoon-scale work, 1:1 drawings are an accessible way to try out, explore, and fine-tune ideas. Initially, drawings can help save a lot of time as a design and exploration tool and, in the end, serve as accurate layout lines and cut lines. It is far easier and less wasteful to be adventurous with your drawings than it is with your carving. We want to encourage spontaneity in our work, but the more inclusive the drawing or drawings are, the closer the idea will be to becoming a reality. Maybe we can help foster these moments of creative spontaneity by striving to have more clear and calm thoughts, making room and space in our lives for the bolt of inspirational lightning to strike. The more drawing practice you get, the better you become, and the better you become, the more you realize you should get more practice.

With confident layout lines, stock can be removed in a very accurate and efficient way with a saw. With this spoon, I am choosing to use the bandsaw for all the rough-out work. The bandsaw is a unique machine that is capable of cutting everything from freehand curves to long, straight rip cuts.

STARTING THE SPOON (top to bottom): *Piece of holly wood. Sketching the spoon on the wood. Removing stock with the bandsaw.*

ABOUT THE BANDSAW

Only in the last two hundred years or so have bandsaws been available. And within really only the last twenty years have machines of this kind been readily available to and designed especially for hobbyists and small shops. They are great tools, indispensable for small sculptural work, and a versatile addition to any tool collection or garage. Bandsaws have the unique ability among machines to cut both curves as well as straight lines.

Essentially, for spoons work, the bandsaw can replace the bow saw. While it is nowhere near as mobile and foolproof as the bow saw—and it should be noted that there are some cuts that are much better suited to the bow saw—the bandsaw is capable of extremely accurate cuts on small parts, with minimal clamping or holding necessary and all with a fraction of the effort required when working with other more traditional saws.

Whenever I am learning about a new machine or even trying to explain the use of a familiar one, one of the first things that I think is important to convey is the necessity to grasp the basic workings of the machine before you attempt to use it. Take account of the parts that move and understand the direction they go in.

This way, you understand the principal forces in action with the tool; you will know where not to be when using the machine, and in which direction your workpiece will fly if there is a problem and you lose control of your work. Before you turn it on, make sure you know how to turn it off. Plan for the worst and expect the best is my kind of approach.

With a bandsaw, the basic working principle of the machine is that a drive wheel moves a continuous, toothed steel belt or band around a second wheel, like a pulley. Both wheels spin in the same plane. The cutting force of the machine is directed into a worktable that is situated under the downward-rotation side of the belt. Therefore the force of the machine is directed down. Unlike a lot of other woodworking machines, that means the force of the downward motion of the blade is keeping the workpiece in place during that cut by literally forcing it into the table. Bandsaws don't kick back like table saws do, but they can "catch" if the blade gets twisted in a piece of wood. Also, cutting round or cylindrical work is most safely accomplished with some type of clamping tactic that can compensate for tangential forces trying to rotate the round at the

BANDSAW

beginning and end of the cut. By and large, bandsaws are safe, extremely useful, and fun tools to use. The more you understand and are able to intuit the forces that are exerted on a piece of wood during the work, the more skill you will develop with the bandsaw and the closer you will be able to rough-cut work to the final shape that you desire.

Get extra blades, because bandsaw blades get dull. It is much better to spend the time changing a dull, worn-out blade than to push and burn through one last cut. As with other tools, a dull bandsaw is a very dangerous tool to use. Dull blades tend to generate a lot of heat and collect pitch, which in turn generates more heat buildup in a rapidly degenerative cycle. Dull blades also require more user force to push through a cut. Struggling to push against a dull blade is asking for trouble. Just change the blade.

Generally, in choosing blades, the narrower the blade from front to back, the tighter the possible radius it will make. Blades that are ¼ in (6 mm) are more than sufficient for spoons work and capable of very tight cuts. Very

hard, dense woods tend to cut better with blades that have more teeth; softer, more fibrous woods, or heavy resaw cuts (the types of cuts used to make boards or planks) work better with blades that have fewer teeth.

Operationally, bandsaws can be used to make almost any cut imaginable. They can be used freehand or with the aid of jigs or fences. Stop cuts or cuts that don't extend all the way through a shape are also possible. For instance, sharp inside corner cuts can be accomplished by first creating a relief cut to the depth of the desired inside corner, then making consecutive cuts, one from each side, to reveal the shape. This way the blade is freed up at the bottom of the cut as the waste material is removed. Backing out of a cut is also possible while the machine is running by going slowly, retracing the line of the cut, and taking great care not to pull the blade from its proper position from inside its guides.

Bandsaw blades can break. This releases all the tension on the saw blade, usually in one loud bang, which can be quite frightening, even more so because you will probably be really concentrating intensely on making a good cut when the blade breaks! Stay as calm as possible, turn the machine off, and wait for it to completely stop spinning before you open the machine up or reach in to remove the broken blade.

The safety advice is simple: Don't have any body part directly in line with the cut path. Ask yourself, "If I were to slip, what direction would I be moving in?" Make sure that your fingers are not pushing along a path that crosses the blade. Remember, the blade itself won't jump at you; it is fairly fixed. You have to be doing something that could unexpectedly lurch a body part into the blade. If the cut that you want to make puts your fingers too close to harm's way for your comfort level, use a push stick to guide your workpiece past the blade. Make sure that your workpiece is firmly in contact with the machine table before starting a cut.

Finally, pay attention to your feed rate. The speed at which you are trying to work will also have an effect on how tight of a curve you can cut. By taking your time around a small radius, the blade will have more of a chance to clear dust from the cut and make its way around without binding or overheating. You will hear a difference in the way the blade sounds if your cut radius is too tight, and you will also begin to smell if the wood begins to burn. Burning is not good during a cut. Generally it is a sign that your blade is overloaded. Back off, back out, or just cut straight ahead if you are really stuck. Keep in the back of your mind that you can always turn a bandsaw off if you really don't like what is happening during a cut.

CUTTING OUT THE SPOON FORM

First, I cut out the top view. If I am careful, and plan the path, I can make it all the way around in one cut. Then I lay out the side projection. With this spoon I am leaving the top very flat, which I like to do with measuring spoons. The flat edge makes it easier to grade the amount of whatever the bowl of the spoon is holding. Also, the flat top allows me to use the entire thickness of this piece of holly to create a generous 1-cup (240-ml) spoon.

As the blank gets flipped to its side, it is evident that we are not only drawing but also cutting on curved

surfaces. There are a couple of ways of dealing with this. In essence, you could tape the top-view cut scraps back on and use that edge to cut from, or you could use a curved jig or carriage system. Or you can freehand it, which I recommend for this type of spoon-making work. As long as there are two points of contact between the workpiece and the machine table, the cut is still quite safe. Even if there are not two points, as in this first cut at the top of the bowl, I can accomplish the cut by taking care to cut only in one axis at a time. The fingers of my right hand reference a consistent distance to the table. I make sure not to twist the workpiece into the blade. Rather, I swing through the cut.

As I am able and it doesn't matter to the symmetry of the cut, I try to find that second point, slowly resting the workpiece into position. Here the handle end finds the table to provide some stability to finish the back cut.

FINISHING CUTTING OUT THE SPOON

With the top-view cut and side-view cut finished, we now concentrate on

CUTTING OUT THE SPOON FORM (top to bottom): Drawing the side cut line for the spoon. Cutting out the rest of the form. Finishing the profile cut (note the handle resting on the bandsaw's work table). (Opposite): With careful attention to resistance and the feed rate, the bandsaw is an incredibly accurate tool.

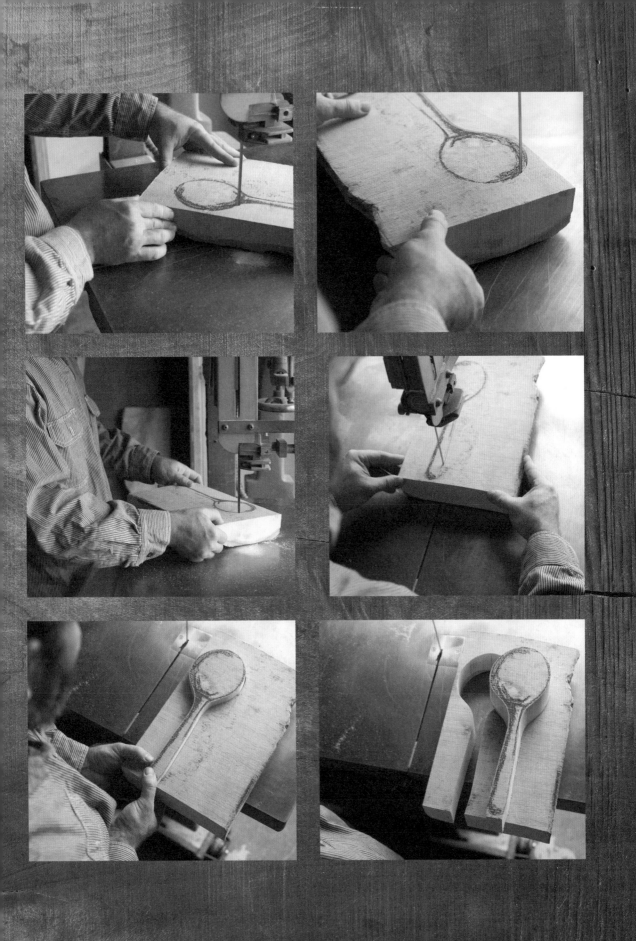

the corners. I measure off each surface an equal amount with my "finger marking gauge," which will give me fairly good, consistent guidelines to cut to. This is basically a 45-degree cut taken off all the edges of the spoon blank. This is the most difficult cutting technique on the bandsaw used for this project, and the most prone to binding up a blade, so use great caution, go slowly, and don't try to take a lot off all in one pass until you understand how to make the cuts.

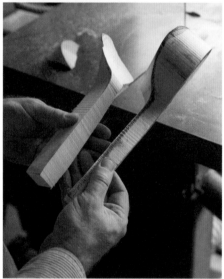

I orient the corner that I'm going to cut toward the bottom to move the point of force that the saw exerts on the workpiece as low to the table as possible. Then, making sure that at least one point remains in contact with the table, I tilt the blank 45 degrees and slowly begin to trace the layout lines with the blade.

I am in the habit of leaving a bit more material around the neck area of a spoon, which I prefer to shape using finer methods. It is also a convenient place to exit these corner cuts.

FINISHING CUTTING OUT THE SPOON (top to bottom): The top view. The side view. Cutting around the spoon with the bandsaw.

TRIMMING AWAY THE EXCESS

I cut front to back, back of the handle to the front. And opposite side of the blade, front to back, and back to front. This keeps my hands out of the way of the blade and leaves a little extra at the neck to be able to sculpt into a nice transition.

Take small controlled cuts where the exit is clear and your hands don't need to get too close to the blade. Don't try to force a cut too quickly. With a little care, almost all your outside curves' rough work can be done with the bandsaw.

THE ROUGHED-OUT SPOON

Rotary tools come in all different shapes and sizes, electric versions are now available at virtually every hardware store, and the selection of bits and burrs is staggering. I am using an abrasive tungsten carbide, medium-grit bit with a pneumatic die grinder. Aside from the noise, air tools are inexpensive to purchase and operate and generally very safe. They are restricted only by your ability to produce enough compressed air.

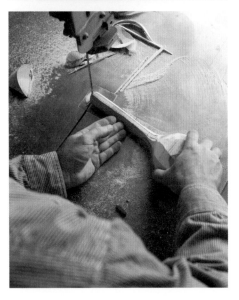

TRIMMING AWAY THE EXCESS (top to bottom):
Trimming around the handle. Trimming the back of the bowl. Trimming the end of the handle.

the **ROUGHED-OUT SPOON**

USING THE BURR TO SHAPE THE SPOON

A good rule of thumb with bit or burr selection is that the harder the material you are carving, the finer the abrasive should be. This burr in particular is easy to control through a variety of wood densities and different grain configurations and is quick to remove stock. I think about this kind of burr as a rotary rasp. Here I begin to refine the outside curves by starting work removing all the high points.

The main bit of safety advice that I have with these types of tools is to watch out for your work-holding thumb. Fast-spinning burrs have a way of driving themselves right around the top of a curve and on to the other side to your awaiting fingers. Also, these kinds of tools can wind themselves up in your clothing, so wear an apron. You can wear work gloves, or another mode of prevention is to get in the habit of working edges and curves downhill toward you and against the rotation of the tool. Work to a point or an apex rather than all the way over

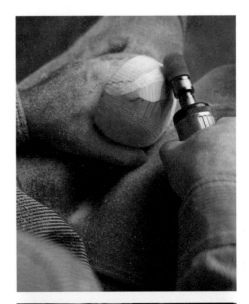

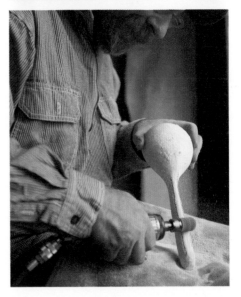

*USING THE BURR TO SHAPE THE SPOON
(top to bottom): Using the burr on the back of the spoon bowl. Drawing an axis line down the spine of the spoon. Working the edges, using the axis line on the back of the handle.*

from one side to the other. Definitely set up a vacuum capable of catching the wood dust that you are going to create. At some point as you work, you should have the sense that you are affecting the flow of the shape of the spoon, and you should be able to recognize your progress with the stock removal. Your tool should be spinning just fast enough to be removing material but not fast enough to burn your workpiece.

I like to develop an axis as a point of reference. Often, a simple chalk line will help me recognize areas that I think need work and help me better see the shape within. Not that symmetry needs to be a rule, perhaps just that the spoon shape really lends itself to this bilateral type of configuration both visually and structurally. I find that understanding this division helps me create shapes that I think are more sophisticated—not necessarily more complicated, just better resolved.

BEGINNING ON THE INSIDE CURVES

With the outside of the spoon well established, here I start the inside curves work with the same tool and bit. I have chalked in the top to better illustrate the carving process. My goal is to carve the bowl down to create an even wall thickness of about ¼ in (6 mm), which I check with my fingers for consistency.

SANDING

A fairly new addition to the rotary tool options are small inflatable sanding heads. The air bladder inflates into an abrasive sleeve by means of a small hand pump. This soft head is more prone to follow contours than it is to create new ones, making them very efficient at sanding complex curves. Inflatable heads come in both cylinder and domed shapes in a variety of sizes.

I begin the sanding work with the outside of the shape, taking great

BEGINNING ON THE INSIDE CURVES (top): Marking the bowl with chalk. (Bottom, left to right): Hollowing out the bowl. Checking the bowl's even wall thickness.

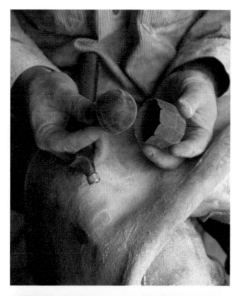

care to refine and smooth any inconsistencies. With the inflatable cylindrical sanding head and some coarse sandpaper, I remove high spots and sweeten all the curves. When I finish this sanding stage, I want the outside shape to be perfect; no further shaping should be necessary.

Now sanding can begin on the inside of the bowl, the inside curves. The domed head inflatable sander with coarse sandpaper makes quick work of refining this inside shape. I am careful to work toward myself and off an edge only against the rotation of the tool. Otherwise, the sandpaper has the potential to catch this trailing edge and shred itself. This is perhaps the most frustrating aspect of using these sanding sleeves. This will happen to you more than once as you learn how to use them. My best advice is to prepare for this eventuality and have extra paper sleeves on hand. My next goal is to remove all tool marks and leave the bowl a consistent $1/8$ to $3/16$ in (3 mm to 5 mm) thick.

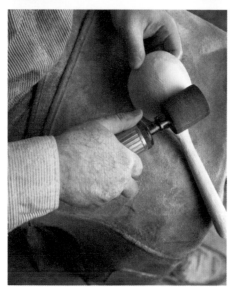

SANDING (top to bottom): An inflatable bladder and sanding head. Smoothing the inside curves of the bowl with the domed sanding head. Smoothing the outside curves of the spoon with a cylindrical sanding head.

FINE-TUNING THE SPOON

In the end I will re-mark my general axis and the big transitional shapes that I am working toward and fine-tune the whole form, bit by bit, until I am satisfied.

Outside curves get a medium sand, followed by the same for the inside curves. This back-and-forth method, inside to outside, helps me work toward the final form without going too far in one aspect.

Look at your shapes more than once. Get up, take a break, come back with fresh eyes; often you will see something that you have previously overlooked. I think this is an important step in learning the language of making shapes that are new to you—the time for reflection. Giving your body and muscle memory the chance to absorb and settle can help to better internalize what has been done and, in turn, what needs to happen.

SOAKING THE SPOON

When I am satisfied with this being the final shape of my spoon, I soak it

FINE-TUNING THE SPOON (top to bottom): Working on the transitional shapes, marking the edges of the bowl as a guide. Re-marking the axis. Sanding to refine the edges and transitions.

in water. The water in this case helps expose problem spots in the carving. After the spoon has been allowed to dry, you will notice many raised areas, nicks, and scratches that you didn't notice before.

The whole spoon will seem quite a bit rougher. This is called "raising the grain." We raise it to be able to better refine it. By identifying problem spots in the surface, we can sand them out with ever finer grades of abrasive papers before we begin the oiling process. The goal is to create a smooth, resilient surface that is a pleasure to use and capable of being cleaned well after use.

FINISHING

I like to do a final hand-sand, using sandpaper that is about 400 grit. There is something special about really feeling the entire piece with your hand. Making sure that it feels good to hold is a significant requirement to meet before a spoon should be called done. There is an old woodworking adage that says the final polish of a piece should be done with the skin on the palm of your hand,

SOAKING THE SPOON (top to bottom):
One last look before soaking. Soaking the spoon in clean water. The spoon post-soaking shows areas that need more attention.

implying that a craftsperson should finish the work by caressing it. It should be the kind of thing that you can experience with your eyes closed. On one level, it is important to engage and satisfy as many senses as possible, but this also helps to describe a level of intimacy possible only between the maker and the object. It is what has gone into creating this feeling that I think transcends the piece and the work itself—not just that it is smooth.

Is it done? Are we finished? The spoon should be refined to a point of satisfaction and beauty so that it can be handed off, given—both in object and in sentiment—from one person to the next, creating an ongoing experience of transference. Not that such a lofty purpose should intimidate you— far from it. A simple act of love need not be made into a grand gesture to be powerful, nor do things need to be perfect to come from the heart.

Signing or decorating can be a way of further differentiating your work. Beyond striving to let the shapes speak for themselves, personalizing something can be a way to further connect. This kind of embellishment

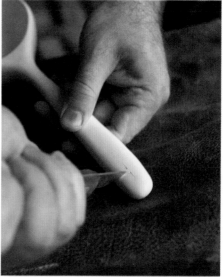

FINISHING (top to bottom): *Final hand-sanding. Decorating the handle, using a stab knife. Oiling the spoon.*

need not be an advertisement or an overt statement. Often small gestural marks are sufficient and can be quite moving.

The stab knife is a great tool for beginners and veteran carvers alike. As its name suggests, it makes its cut by applying a stabbing pressure through the blade rather than slicing or cutting with it. Essentially, a stab knife creates regular, wedge-shaped indentations that can be formed into patterns.

A small pattern for good luck at the end of the handle of this spoon means the carving work is done and the spoon is ready for oil.

In the end, it seemed only right to return this spoon back to its original block, as a gesture of how far it came along its path and a nod to the foundation from which it was cut. It was like fitting the last piece of a puzzle. I felt the magnetic need to put them back together. This wonderful kind of juxtaposition fascinates me—positive and negative, smooth and rough. It seems a very simple yet powerful concept that one might need the other. There is enough material left to make at least one more spoon, but perhaps this pairing best exemplifies the story of this spoon and its origin more than any number of words ever could.

EPILOGUE

After creating this book I am very thankful for the small but enriching journey that the spoons have taken me on and the unique gift of perspective gained. In creating all the spoons for the compendium, I discovered that there is a tremendous joy and satisfaction to be found in the investigation of a new shape or the personal discovery of a new form—much like the joy and richness of learning a new language. I was reminded that the practice of spoon making provides an endless source of fun and excitement that comes from learning and sharing, that work itself can be liberating, and that it can all happen no farther away than one's front porch.

Design is indeed all around us and offers endless potential. Who we are and where we have come from can only add to the rising conversation about the value of creative culture. Ultimately, spoon making is a very accessible way to actively participate in this conversation.

Not everything can be handmade in our world today. There is enormous pressure to manufacture things faster and faster all the time, and there is a greater need to make more money with the energy that we expend on the things that we do make. Of course, some objects have become so sophisticated that they can no longer be made by hand. We can easily envision a future in which there may be even fewer reasons for things to be made this way. Sad though it may seem, there is nothing inherently wrong with greater productivity or technological advancement—far from it. Some of these advances allow an entirely new type of creativity to happen that might not otherwise exist. That in itself should be acknowledged as a great artistic achievement. As long as that progress doesn't come at the expense of the human spirit or to the detriment of our environment, I don't see the point of trying to resist these changes.

Realizing that this is the way of our new world—a world of three-dimensional print- ers—and that the technical revolution is signaling a great paradigm shift in our lives, should make handmade objects even more special. I think these artisanal kinds of endeavors should be recognized for the increasingly unique value that they hold in today's world. They *are* the arts. They are the artifacts that we use to communicate soulfulness, beauty, and meaning to others. They connect us to our environment, they connect us to each other. They can characterize and define culture and cultural movement. They are the things that we use to speak about the power of human spirit and nourish the undeniable need to be creative—not just productive, but creative.

With this book, through both the writing of it and the wood carving, I hope I've encouraged others to make a place for this kind of work in their lives. Spoons are as useful today as they were thousands of years ago. Carved spoons can be uniquely poetic and also a completely accessible and fun introduction to woodcarving, tool making, and design in general.

Whether you are supporting an artist or seek to become one yourself, whether you are a collector, a cook, a longtime woodworker, or a novice craftsperson, spoon carving can be more than just a diversion. It is an open, welcoming tradition, arguably among the oldest and furthest reaching. Although the craft is ancient, now more than ever it is a way to apply yourself in an especially useful, timeless, and relevant way. With all that said, I hope you will join me.

ACKNOWLEDGMENTS

It is pure illusion that we are ever "self-made" or that we can be entirely autonomous. Nothing in this world can be accomplished alone. Many people are responsible both directly and indirectly for the making of this book.

First, I need to thank Chronicle Books for their tireless efforts in an uncertain world to fight the good fight, and in their collective belief in projects like this book. Special thanks go to Lorena Jones, who first recognized the potential in me to write and then had the patience to see the book through. My vision for this project is as much her vision. Also to designer Jennifer Tolo Pierce, who helped create an environment and feeling for my work to exist in. Without either of you, this book would not have been possible.

Seth and Kendra Smoot need more than just acknowledgment. It is their expertise, energy, and friendship that have made this simple narrative more than just visually compelling, but wholly beautiful. It is truly a pleasure to collaborate with such talented and dedicated people, and I owe both of them a great debt of gratitude.

Dan Votke has been instrumental throughout this writing process in keeping our small shop going. His desire to learn and the amount of elbow grease that he has contributed are an inspiration to me.

I would be remiss if I didn't thank Sam Hamilton at MARCH in San Francisco for taking an early interest in, and encouraging my efforts. She is an original. Her savvy and elegance are truly aspirational, not to mention that she has been a joy to work with, which I think says a lot about both her business and her intentions as well.

Thanks to our neighbor Matt Greene, who was generous enough to allow us to shoot pictures on his property and kind enough to overlook the mess I made in the corner of his beautiful barn.

Thanks also to Westwind Orchard for their generosity and dedication to a life better lived.

But mostly, in the day-to-day work and for believing in me and picking me up when I am down, I owe the most thanks to Kelly Zaneto. Her strength, determination, and encouragement have done much to make this project become a reality. Since the beginning of this book project we have begun a family of our own, and our daughter, Violet, has become the light of both our lives. Through all of this, Kelly has helped me juggle and navigate the technological maelstrom of word processing and computing. She has been my manager, editor, and cheerleader, and the sounding board for my many musings. Quite remarkably, for as busy as we are, she has created time in my life for this type of focus when there definitely has not been any time. Kelly, I love you.

A heartfelt thanks goes out to you all!

INDEX